"Your endorsement."

I'm confident in the power of this book—and the unique resources provided here—to help you find the best possible career for who you are. Your success is our most important endorsement. —GARY BURNISON

LOSE THE RESUME

LAND THE JOB

BY GARY BURNISON

Book design by RossMadrid Group
Illustrations by Brett Ryder

Published by John Wiley & Sons, Inc., Hoboken, New Jersey
Published simultaneously in Canada

For general information about our other products and services, please contact our Customer Care Department within the United States at (800) 762-2974, outside the United States at (317) 572-3993 or fax (317) 572-4002.

Wiley publishes in a variety of print and electronic formats and by print-on-demand. Some material included with standard print versions of this book may not be included in e-books or in print-on-demand. If this book refers to media such as a CD or DVD that is not included in the version you purchased, you may download this material at http://booksupport.wiley.com. For more information about Wiley products, visit www.wiley.com.

Library of Congress Cataloging-in-Publication Data

Names: Burnison, Gary, 1961- author.
Title: Lose the resume : land the job / by Gary Burnison.
Description: Hoboken, New Jersey : John Wiley & Sons, Inc., [2018] |
    Identifiers: LCCN 2017051510 (print) | LCCN 2017054519 (ebook) | ISBN
    9781119475255 (pdf) | ISBN 9781119475231 (epub) | ISBN 9781119475200 (pbk.)
Subjects: LCSH: Job hunting. | Vocational guidance.
Classification: LCC HF5382.7 (ebook) | LCC HF5382.7 .B88 2018 (print) | DDC
    650.14--dc23
LC record available at https://lccn.loc.gov/2017051510

Printed in the United States of America

V10008979_032719

LOSE THE LAND THE JOB RESUME

ALMOST EVERYONE GETS IT WRONG.
THIS IS HOW YOU CAN GET IT RIGHT. **GARY BURNISON**

TABLE OF CONTENTS

To everyone who hates his or her boss.

Early one morning, as I drove to work along the Pacific Coast Highway— the sun glistening off the ocean to my right—traffic suddenly slowed to a crawl. Several cars stopped in the median of a six-lane highway where cars normally move at a steady fifty-five miles per hour. One man stepped out of his truck and stared at the ground. As I rolled slowly past, I couldn't believe what I was seeing: A skunk had a plastic soda cup stuck on its head. It had obviously jammed its snout to the bottom of the cup to get the last drops of sweet liquid, and now it was stuck. Scampering frantically left and right, the skunk shook its head violently back and forth in a fruitless attempt to dislodge the cup. Timidly, the man circled the animal—clearly at the crossroads of whether to be the hero of the helpless or a victim of the clueless. Eventually, an animal-control officer arrived and safely removed the soda cup from the poor animal's head. But the image of the man and the skunk was burned into my memory.

Far too many people today feel helpless and clueless when it comes to getting their next job. And too often they act just like the skunk. They focus on what they believe is a "sweet" opportunity without considering the fit. And just like the skunk, they find themselves stuck. They're in the wrong environment; the culture is not a fit. They're working for the wrong boss, who is never going to champion them to gain the learning experiences that will expand their skill set. And all they can do is shake their head back and forth, wondering how they can get out of this mess.

How can I get a new job? What's it going to take? What should my resume say? How do I go about this process? People at the earliest stages of their career are not the only ones asking these questions. I hear them from people at all levels, even those who have two or three decades of professional experience.

Their stories of frustration and confusion are similar. I can't help but have empathy. But honestly, in the back of my mind I'm thinking something is terribly wrong here— unfortunately, with them. Their entire approach is just plain wrong.

In my thirty-five years of professional life, including the last decade as CEO of a public company, I have been continuously shocked by the naiveté of people when it comes to their career. From the supposed most sophisticated to the least experienced, from Fortune 500 board members and seasoned executives to college seniors, people are confounded by how to find their next "gig." Not knowing what to do, they resort to the old standby: "Let me send you my resume," which has become as meaningless a cliché as "Let's do lunch." When you say it, you know you're never going to have lunch. The same goes for your offer to email your resume. Unless someone genuinely wants to hear from you, your resume isn't going anywhere.

That's why you need to lose the resume to land the right job. Yes, you still need to have a resume, but don't expect it to be more than a calling card, a conversation opener. Unfortunately, people think their resume accounts for 90 percent of getting a new job, when actually it's only 10 percent. No wonder sending out resumes isn't getting people where they want or need to go!

"Let me send you my resume" has become as meaningless a cliché as "Let's do lunch."

While it's true that almost anyone with a decent education and some experience can get a job, finding the *right* job is not easy. In fact, it has never been harder. Forget unemployment rates that might not seem so bad these days; most unemployment figures mask the fact that the combination of technology and a merciless global economy has made it almost impossible to find work that offers the compensation we want or purpose we need. In survey after survey, it's the same complaints: Wage growth isn't happening, motivation is down, and job stability is vanishing. Here's a ridiculous stat: Half of U.S. workers have a pay rate that fluctuates sharply every month—by almost 30 percent.

Yet the only way out of this trap is to engage in a job-search process that people never expect to be so arduous or so long. If you are like most people, you will start out by making the critical mistake of waiting for opportunities to come to you. Given that an average of 250 resumes are received for every corporate-job opening—the first 200 typically land just seconds after the job is posted—this approach is patently passive and illogical. And when you fail to gain any traction, you tend to send out more resumes. You feel stuck—like a victim.

As time goes on, you begin to doubt yourself. If you lose heart, desperation sets in. Soon you'll lose all perspective about yourself and where you want to work. You take any job rather than languish in a position you don't like anymore. Or you quit before getting another job—and that's the number-one mistake to avoid, because you need to have a job to get a job. When you're "marketing yourself," you must eliminate every red flag that could sink your career.

> **People think their resume accounts for 90 percent of getting a new job, when actually it's only 10 percent.**

This is the kind of straight talk you're going to get in this book, so that you're no longer at the mercy of the odds that obviously are not in your favor. To break this cycle, you need to change your strategy, to shift to a more active and calculated approach.

The analogy I use is surfing, which exemplifies my life philosophy. Everyone, I believe, gets a number of "waves" in life—some enormous, some much smaller. The trick is to know when and how hard to paddle when your wave appears, how to position yourself for success—when to bail before the wave crashes on you, and when to ride all the way to shore. One thing is certain: You never look down. Look up, look forward, take flight. This book is about creating more waves for yourself, creating the opportunities that will expand your learning, connect with your purpose, and bring more meaning to what you do.

This approach requires action and hard work. You have to understand who you are, your strengths and weaknesses, your purpose, and what motivates you. You need to know the kind of environment you thrive in, even the type of boss you work best with. You must have a plan that targets where you want to work, and you have to network to make the strategic connections that will help you get to those employers. Most important, the effort and details must be at a level that makes all your past job searches seem like sixth-grade homework. For example, "investigating" a company's culture doesn't mean just checking out a company review site. It may require finding and listening to recordings of the earnings calls that public companies make every quarter. Indeed, the detail that's needed is almost always what people skip over.

Fortunately, you have help. At Korn Ferry, we have shown 8 million executives how to achieve their career goals. As the world's largest executive recruiter, we place one professional in a job every three minutes. While we've been known for executive search for more than fifty years, our company today is much broader: We are the leader in talent development and organizational development. More than half of our business involves developing executives and professionals and advising the world's leading companies on their organizational strategy. (Full disclosure: Korn Ferry also offers individuals looking for work a new tool called **KFAdvance.com** to guide the process. But even our coaches will tell you that you still have to do the hard work.)

The research behind recruiting, hiring, and retention is fascinating. Our company houses its own "Institute," with PhDs from the world's top universities. The assessment tests they've developed boggle the mind with their ability to accurately forecast anyone's future management behavior. This expertise—along with that from myself and nearly 8,000 Korn Ferry colleagues around the globe—is brought to bear in these pages and distilled into simplified exercises and assessments that can help you.

You'll have access to insights and tools that until now were available only to senior executives. And we'll clue you in to exactly what recruiters are thinking when someone becomes a job opening's 100th candidate to talk about being a "team player," instead of demonstrating an understanding of how to collaborate.

With this encyclopedic knowledge and your newly efficient approach, you'll see the odds moving in your favor. It's like *Moneyball*, the best-selling book and Brad Pitt movie, which describes the radical approach the Oakland A's took to build a winning baseball team. Instead of fielding high-priced superstar talent, they made strategic choices that radically increased their chances of winning. Consider this your *Moneyball* playbook. Step by step, you'll learn what can meaningfully improve the chance that you'll win.

Lose the Resume, Land the Job is organized into three parts. The first is about knowing yourself—your strengths and weaknesses, motivation, behavior, and personality traits. We'll get you there with a series of personality tests developed from our world-class IP (intellectual property) that, trust me, you can't outsmart. The tests may reveal traits you didn't know you had—and recruiters definitely will discover.

Then we'll show you how to match those skills with the specific companies that need them, instead of wasting time with those that don't. For this, you'll be doing detective work into companies and their HR teams that you never thought possible. Finally, you'll learn how to present your story through, yes, your now expertly crafted resume, your carefully manicured online and social-media presence, and the all-important face-to-face (or Skype) interview. When the job offer comes, we'll give you insight into what companies are thinking about in terms of both money and nonmonetary issues.

Ultimately, you'll need to face the fact that job hunting in the twenty-first century requires a focus and dedication you didn't know you had.

Does any of this sound like something you're willing to do? If so, then by the end of this book, you will have far more in your job-search arsenal than just your resume. You'll have a holistic approach grounded in who you are, where you can be most successful, and the story you tell to forge a connection with a prospective employer. And that's so much more empowering than merely getting your next job. It's the key to your future success. •

> **Job hunting in the twenty-first century requires a focus and dedication you didn't know you had.**

YOUR WAKE-UP CALL

ONE

YOUR WAKE-UP CALL

"**I**'m getting a new job.**"** You've been telling your family and friends this so many times they're ready to run away when you say it again. Reminders are on hand-scrawled notes on the refrigerator and clutter your iPhone calendar. What drove you to make this move has ranged over the years, but pick one: Your boss is a nightmare; your company is posting losses; you don't feel appreciated. Or on a more positive note, you know you've done amazing work and deserve a fantastic opportunity—the kind that Jane, your cheery neighbor, just got with seemingly half your effort. The thoughts won't leave your head: *I'm going to get a new job. Today! I'm not kidding.*

That means it's time to look in the bathroom mirror, splash some cold water on your face, and ask yourself:

Now what?

There is an entire industry that will give you a simple, pat answer: Polish that resume and start searching online. You've no doubt seen these firms. Out of virtually nowhere has sprung a resume-writing sector that numbers 4,000 to 6,000 companies in the United States alone. While most are one-person operations, the biggest names have become corporate giants with their own apps and email reminders. These firms will tell you they employ the best artificial intelligence known to humankind to make sure no job opening escapes your notice, and that every line in your resume is just what the HR department wants. The message through these rose-colored glasses is universal: A few clicks (and perhaps a small fee) and it's off to the job interviews!

All of this, of course, ignores the realities of how difficult job hunting has become. The change has nothing to do with macro-economic factors such as artificial intelligence or advanced robotics. Rather, the job-search process has changed radically. Going back thirty or forty years, it was simple. You looked in the help-wanted ads of your local newspaper and searched for an opening that matched your skill set. The job market was largely restricted to a certain city or region, and the candidates you competed against were local to that region. The world wasn't as specialized as it is today. You wrote a letter or made a phone call, and if the employer liked you, the job was yours. It wasn't unheard of back then to get a job in a day, especially in a small city.

The process today, of course, is far broader and a lot more democratic. Thanks to the Internet and career sites such as the omnipresent LinkedIn, job postings are easy to find. As a matter of routine, nearly every global organization also posts its job opportunities on its own career pages to cast as wide a net as possible. What sounds like good news, though, is actually the problem. The floodgates are so open now that *anyone* can apply for a job anywhere, even if that person is not remotely qualified. And many people do apply blindly, burying the hopes of the truly qualified.

Sure, you can improve your odds by including keywords on your resume or in your LinkedIn profile that search engines will pick up, but it's still absurdly hard for even great candidates to stand out in this sea of eager beavers. The whole process has become sad. People put enormous care into writing their resumes—right down to using the preferred Times New Roman font—only to have them go nowhere when they're submitted online or emailed. ●

The Unspoken Truth

If you're only sending out your resume, you're not going to get hired.

THE BLUNT TRUTH

Over the past several years I've received thousands of resumes, unsolicited and from people I don't know. And guess what: They rarely go anywhere. Most of the time, I don't even open the document. That might strike you as harsh or even unfair, but here's what I know about many other CEOs and senior executives: They're not opening your resume either.

This brings me back to our core advice to "lose the resume"—figuratively speaking. Of course, you need to have a resume. But you should keep your resume in perspective. Your resume alone won't land the next job for you, and it certainly won't advance your career along the trajectory that will get you where you truly want to go.

In fact, if you just send out resumes, you have already lost! Consider these statistics: Of the 250 resumes going out for every corporate job, the initial screening typically eliminates 98 percent of job seekers, and only 2 percent will

> Simply sending out resumes blindly means you've already lost!

even get an interview. These numbers don't make it into most resume-writing guides. Then again, this isn't meant to be another one of those books. This book serves a different purpose: to enlighten you about the rules of engagement—how to think, act, present yourself, and tell your unique story—so that you can win.

Make no mistake: Getting a job is the ultimate contest between you and every other candidate. Your mindset needs to be that of a true competitor. Ex-NBA star Allen Iverson said in his Hall of Fame induction speech that, as he learned in sports, "If it's me or you, it's me." If your mindset is anything less, you're not going to achieve your goals. To win, you need a sense of urgency. Once you commit to making a career move, you must put yourself on a deadline. Act as if your job is going to be eliminated in six months! Suddenly, your whole mindset changes. You vow to take control of your professional destiny before it's too late. You have to act quickly, because another unspoken truth is this: It's better to have a job when you're looking for a new one. You become single-minded in your pursuit of the next opportunity. This includes, as you'll soon see, doing the hard work of looking within to assess your strengths and weaknesses, what motivates you, where you fit in, and the contributions you can make to your next employer.

I have to tell you that as a CEO, I always find that the candidates who show a great willpower and drive to land a job—and who avoid the inertia of searching lamely—are the ones who make great employees. Frankly, I would never want to hire

What you've done is not what counts. Who you are and what you will do for them matter most.

someone who views work as just a job. I'm looking for people who equate work with meaning, with purpose—their life goals and destination. These are the 20 percent of people who account for 80 percent of what the organization accomplishes. They aren't going through the motions of what's required. They are invariably "all in," because they equate their job with purpose.

So before you even think of your resume, you must first be introspective. That starts with knowing what you want and why you want it—what inspires and motivates you—and knowing which type of environment and culture will enable you to thrive. ●

GETTING A CLUE

Most people, however, have no idea what they really want or where they'd be best suited. On top of that, they lie—all the time and especially to themselves. Needless to say, this is not a winning combination.

Without a handle on your strengths and accomplishments, as well as an understanding of your blind spots, your weaknesses, and where you need to develop, you will lack clarity in the job search. The heart of the process is finding meaning—your passion and purpose. Far more than the proverbial "following your bliss," passion and purpose ignite performance! This is an unbeatable combination—the motivation and inspiration that drives you to achieve.

I say all this because if you haven't been in the job market lately, you are in for a shock at how rigorously companies try to find truly motivated candidates—and sniff out the punch-the-clockers. I hear comments all the time about the hours upon hours of interviews and assessments companies now put people through. And then all the "I Spy" background checks, reference calls, and social-media snooping.

But these candidates don't realize just how much pressure companies are under to perform in today's business climate—and how critical good hiring has become. Slow-performing companies can be crushed by competitors that are able to use technology to scale up quickly, or eaten alive by activist investors whose aggressiveness and clout

Faking It

Can you fool companies into thinking you have passion when you don't? Sure, you can try, but some of the greatest research minds have dedicated their lives to perfecting tests that sniff out liars and force candid self-assessments. In one of the bigger breakthroughs in this field, a 2010 University of Barcelona study found that asking people to rank statements instead of grade them brought out the truth. At Korn Ferry, we believe in the "forced-choice" theory of testing. But the bottom line is you will find it easier and a lot more rewarding to reclaim your own passion instead of trying to game the system.

would have been unheard of just a decade ago. In this kind of world, there is no room to miss out on star hires and be stuck with the dregs because of a lousy hiring system.

Our research finds that the cost of replacing a manager six to twelve months after he or she is hired is equal to 2.3 times the person's annual salary. For a senior executive, the replacement cost can well exceed $1 million. More important, companies know that the profits Wall Street wants to see each quarter are largely the product of what we like to call "discretionary energy," basically the extra work and innovation only the most eager employees bring. You hear top executives say it all the time: If they can consistently stiff-arm the drifters and draft the dream team, the company is golden.

So trust me, any organization worth its name has a pretty good chance of finding out if you're a passionless dud—if that's who you are. And it won't matter if you have an amazing pedigree. The good news, however, is that there is passion in all of us, even if your last job squashed it.

My passion is being part of an organization that is transforming an industry. We are creating the new and the different as a people- and organizational-advisory firm. I get out of bed in the morning (before my alarm clock goes off) thinking about what we can do next to achieve our purpose.

In the same way, you need to get in touch with what gets you up and excited at four

> **You need to get in touch with what gets you up and excited at four o'clock in the morning without the alarm.**

o'clock in the morning without the alarm. And don't think Millennials are the only ones motivated by purpose. As I've found in my interactions with people at all levels of organizations (including the one I lead), most desire meaning in what they do. Our research backs this up. In a recent survey of professionals by Korn Ferry, nearly three-quarters (73 percent) cited "work that has purpose and meaning" as their primary driver. When purpose is your motivator, it becomes authentic and tangible in the story you tell about your career thus far, and where you're headed.

Smart companies that have purpose aren't afraid to pound their chest about it and seek only truly purpose-driven employees. (And by the way, be suspicious of those companies that say they have purpose but don't seem to be following through.) The CEO of a large industrial company made this same point as we discussed talent. In on-campus recruiting, on the company's career website, and in every interview for positions at every level, the core message is purpose. This company does not see itself as only manufacturing complex industrial equipment. It sees itself as literally and authentically changing the world by tackling some of the most pressing problems on the planet, from access to electricity to global climate change. If a job applicant doesn't have a genuine passion for the company's overarching purpose, then that person isn't a fit for the culture—no matter how good the person's technical skills are. •

It's All About How You ACT

AUTHENTIC

Truthfully presenting yourself, your experiences, and your background

Whether you're networking with contacts, interacting with a recruiter, or interviewing with a hiring manager, it's all about how you "ACT."

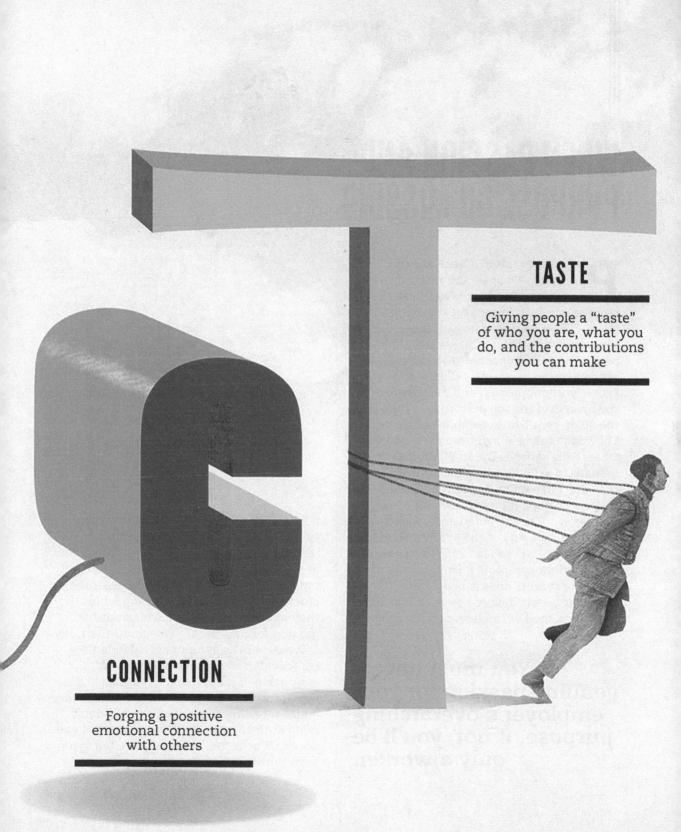

TASTE

Giving people a "taste" of who you are, what you do, and the contributions you can make

CONNECTION

Forging a positive emotional connection with others

WHEN PASSION AND PURPOSE GO MISSING

Purpose. Passion. These are two pretty big P words, and realizing how critical they are in today's "lose the resume" job-hunting era means doing a gut check on your own level of passion. Without strong doses of passion and purpose, it is nearly impossible to be a positive outlier. Performance is mediocre, at best. People without passion and purpose are the inverse of the top performers. They are the 80 percent who accomplish 20 percent. They don't take enough time to figure out what really satisfies them. When they do manage to get a new job, it usually is one they don't like much better than the one they had before. *It's a paycheck*, they tell themselves. They're bored and apathetic.

Do you have any of the symptoms of a passionless career (page 29)? There are, of course, other symptoms. Perhaps one of the more serious ones is bad health. It's true that people devoted to work may eat more junk food, sleep less, and miss the post-work trip to the gym. But aren't they typically the ones who find the time to recoup? Maybe they're up before the crack of dawn—no snooze alarms here!—to get in those five miles and prepare organic chicken salad for lunch. Putting it bluntly, they have the will to live well, and that passion follows them throughout their day.

Whatever the symptoms, a passionless career can lead you into the temptation of quitting. If it does, don't! Job gaps and career interruptions are major red flags for employers. Stay where you are and don't jump at the first thing to come along. If you do, you'll be mired in those same ten symptoms within six months! •

> **You must have a genuine passion for your employer's overarching purpose. If not, you'll be only a worker.**

THE TOP 10
SYMPTOMS OF A PASSIONLESS CAREER

1
YOU'RE ON SNOOZE CONTROL. NO MATTER HOW MUCH SLEEP YOU GET, YOU ARE A YAWN MACHINE

You think the fatigue will make everyone assume you've been up all night working, but you're fooling no one. At home, when the alarm goes off, you treat the snooze button like a pet: always in need of constant tapping.

2
YOU LOVE YOUR COMMUTE

Your train ride in is two hours, but you've become so apathetic at work that it's the best time of your day—the chance to watch the fall leaves from the window or finally finish reading *Moby-Dick*. If you drive, your traffic "nightmare" gives you a great excuse for coming in late—and skipping out early.

3
YOUR COLLEAGUES COULD BE FROM MARS

You've had the same office for a good two years now, and you have never bothered to learn a thing about the person in the office next to yours. It's too far of a walk.

4
LUNCH HOUR IS ANYTHING BUT

You normally never lose track of time. But your lunch time? Sixty minutes never fails to stretch to ninety—and the food isn't even good!

5
YOU HATE SKYPE

Because the camera will reveal that you're nodding off during the conference call's PowerPoint presentation, you decide it's better to just say your password isn't working and phone in.

6
BUT EMAIL IS YOUR FRIEND

You used to call to answer colleagues' questions, but it feels too hard. Emailing lets you put things off. "Sorry for the delay" becomes your mantra. In general, you're less eager to learn any new technology because it means more engagement. Please don't even mention the word "Excel."

7
WHAT COMPETITION?

You haven't used a dime of your budget on industry publications, and the most exciting thing you can recall from the last industry meet-and-greet was watching a guy spill beer on himself.

8
YOUR PERFORMANCE REVIEW LASTED SEVEN MINUTES

Unless they're calling you to complain about your last assignment, your bosses blow you off. Asked in an assessment to bring up your goals, you lie about wanting "to grow" and to help others get ahead.

9
PROMOTIONS ARE FOR LOSERS

After not having one for five years, you've talked yourself into believing they are not possible at your company. But the idea of looking for a new job seems like a lot of work.

10
YOU PRAY— AND I MEAN PRAY—FOR JURY DUTY

Enough said.

THE BOSS PROBLEM

Good Bosses, Bad Bosses: Learning from Both

Good bosses model the behavior they want to see in others. They are rarely teachers; rather, they are lifelong learners who are invested in others' success.

Bad bosses teach you how not to be and, therefore, what to do instead. Ironically, people are more likely to learn about compassion and integrity from the bad boss than from the good one. The reason? They experience directly how horrible it feels to be subjected to a bad boss's behavior.

If you want to jump ship because of a bad boss, don't do it. Let's face it, about 50 percent of people have trouble with their bosses. It's so common that in my business we say people don't leave companies; they leave bosses. The frequent complaints include: The boss doesn't give feedback, doesn't recognize people for what they do, bases promotions more on personality than performance, and so on. All these may be well founded, but here's some advice I like to give: Having a bad boss can actually be a valuable learning experience.

In fact, it is the best way to learn *what not to do* and *how not to act*. The consolation is that you never stay with one boss very long. The boss will move, or you will.

But whether it's harsh feelings about a bad boss or boredom or any other negative emotion that becomes your catalyst for trying to get a new job, you're almost guaranteed to make a wrong move. You need to move *toward* something, not just away from something.

This brings me to a candidate whom I must sadly refer to as "Startup Zach." •

THE TALE OF STARTUP ZACH

Afriend of mine, Jen, brought Startup Zach—as we can call him—to my office one day. By the time he came in, I could only wish we had a time machine, because he was a year too late. Worst of all, he knew it.

Startup Zach had spent most of his career in large financial institutions—highly structured, hierarchical firms. He did well, and his career progressed over the years, but he kept hearing from Jen, who was his neighbor, about a great startup she joined. The more Zach listened to her talk about launching and scaling a business, the more he wanted to try something new. He convinced himself that he, too, was entrepreneurial and could excel in a "flat" organization.

If only he had taken the time to look deeply within himself and recognize what had made him successful where he was. If only he'd talked to a former boss or mentor who could have given him feedback about trying to make such a drastic career move. If only he had done a self-assessment to understand his motivation and his leadership style. Instead, he began moving away from something that was working and became fixated on something he knew nothing about.

Zach was adamant that it was time for a change and startups were the only way to go. Give him credit for one thing: He did a complete makeover, wearing his hair a little longer and dressing down his wardrobe as much as he could at work. He consumed everything he could about the startup world, about incubators and accelerators. He became an expert on Jeff Bezos.

Jen cautioned him: The startup world wasn't as glamorous as he was making it out to be. It wasn't all hoodies and high fives. And it was so different from what he was used to. But Zach wouldn't listen. He convinced himself that his company

executive team, he soon learned, preferred to work virtually.

And then there was lunch—literally wheeled in and set up cafeteria style. Everyone ponied up in a line. "How long has this been going on?" Zach asked, trying to fathom the expense of feeding the entire office every day. "Free food all day," one of his new coworkers said, misunderstanding the question. "You know where the snack closet is?"

While there was undoubtedly a lot of talent in the room, Zach felt he was the only grownup. (In actuality, his lack of self-awareness, which led him to pursue a

If only Zach had taken time to look in the mirror to see exactly who he was.

had held him back. Unfortunately for Zach, he didn't really know himself or his true passion and purpose. He forgot how much he valued hierarchy and boundaries. He overlooked the comfort he found in the clear delineation between roles and responsibilities.

Ultimately, Zach networked his way into a job at a startup—and found out pretty quickly how wrong he was. His first day on the job, the office was half empty. He thought it might have been a holiday he wasn't aware of. But when he asked a coworker—someone half his age dressed in jeans and a hoodie—where everyone was, he got a shrug for an answer. Even the

job that was a poor fit for him, showed his immaturity.)

The hardest part of all was trying to get things done. Zach struggled every day with the ambiguity of the entrepreneurial environment, where jobs and responsibilities often blurred. Without a structure and clear lines of communication, Zach became highly ineffective. After a few days, he woke up from the dream he'd lulled himself into and realized the startup world was a terrible fit for him. There was no one at the startup who was like him, no one who spoke his language. The company knew it, too.

Startup Zach lasted two and a half months. Although he was allowed to resign, the truth is he was fired. That's when he came to see me. "How do I deal with this on my resume?" he asked. And my heart sank.

Zach had indeed dug himself a hole, and it would take a long time and a lot of excavation to get out. The lesson he learned, albeit too late, was he'd forgotten his core values. He ignored the fact that he is best suited to a large, well-established company.

The first thing I advised Zach to do was get in touch with his passion and purpose—what really inspires and motivates him. To do that, we put him through a self-assessment (such as the exercises and assessments in Chapters Two and Three of this book). Based on what the self-assessment showed him, Zach more clearly understood the story he had to tell. It revealed that Zach thrived in a structured environment with clear boundaries, and that he had difficulty managing in ambiguity. It explained a lot about why he was so frustrated by the startup environment.

Realizing at last what he truly wanted, Zach took eight months to get back on track, which hurt him financially and strained his marriage. He ended up back in financial services, a step below where he was before. This is another negative he'll have to overcome, because future employers will want to see career progression, not regression.

But Zach learned the lesson the hard way. Without self-awareness and self-knowledge, he became a prime example of why you should, as the adage says, "Be careful what you wish for." He became the victim of a wish he never should have made. It sounds basic perhaps, but Zach simply didn't understand who he was. •

THE WRONG REASONS TO LOOK FOR WORK

As this sad tale illustrates, people can end up on job searches for incredibly random reasons. What might have happened if Jen was in the STEM business, and Startup Zach became hell-bent on getting into that field, going back to grad school and running up a huge debt in his forties? But to some degree, all this randomness is how many of us, unfortunately, make a lot of decisions in life—and with equal chance of disaster. The best but most uncomfortable analogy is marriage.

In the United States, if 100 couples marry, chances are only 40 to 50 of them will stay together over time. Oddly, the "divorce rate" among new hires and their employers is about the same. Studies show that nearly half (46 percent) of new hires fail within the first eighteen months. The reason cited in nearly nine out of ten cases is "attitude"—a broad term that implies someone was uncooperative or in general didn't "get it." In other words, there was cultural incompatibility.

Our research shows that technical skills alone are not enough for success. You have to fit with the culture. Of course, the majority of people hired want to do well. But they can't, because they feel little or no connection with where they work and what they do. Without passion and purpose, performance can only suffer. That's why people fail—particularly those in more senior positions.

Here is another corollary between the failure of marriages and jobs: People don't know what they want or what suits them best. They aren't self-aware. Often, poor career moves come down to your "job clock" ticking. You've been in one place for X number of years, and suddenly you panic and think you have to make a move. But without a game plan, you jump at the first job, without having thought it through. That's about as wise as deciding to marry the next available person who walks down the street. You'll be heading for the divorce lawyer before you unwrap all the wedding presents.

Or like Zach, you go chasing after an ill-suited opportunity, without evaluating how compatible you and this new position really are. You might be able to pretend for a while that you really do fit in the wrong environment—a round peg happy in a square hole. But before too long, a bad fit rubs in all the wrong places.

Don't do this to yourself. Make moves that are best suited to you—your passion and your purpose. This will elevate your performance. Work in a culture where you fit, and work for a boss you not only like but will also learn from. ●

> Culture fit is as big as technical fit for achieving success.

THE RIGHT REASONS TO LOOK

Many people may not have thought seriously about passion and purpose in terms of their career. Maybe they found it hard to get a job out of college because their skill set was not in demand. Or maybe they were laid off during the Great Recession that followed the 2008 financial crisis and getting any job took precedence over worrying about passion. But that doesn't mean you can't change your career strategy this time around.

It's time to heed the wake-up call and get serious about your career development. For you to improve your chances of being successful—of tapping deep motivations that will be the engine driving your performance—you need to think more deeply about your passion and purpose. This means that before you take one step

Instead of looking to make a jump and land somewhere, you need to be strategic. . . . Think several moves ahead.

externally—by polishing your resume or putting feelers out to your network—you must do the hard work internally.

You need greater self-awareness and self-knowledge of what resonates deeply within. Otherwise you'll go at the career equation without knowing what "X" really is. You'll be solving for the wrong variable, which most of the time means a slightly different title and a little more money. You won't know that at the core of your being, you're hungry to make more of an impact.

When the bell goes off, instead of looking to make a jump and land somewhere, you need to be strategic. This isn't a roll of the dice. It's a game of chess. Think several moves ahead. Your next job should be a "resume builder" that continues a progression of more responsibilities and leading bigger teams. But this will happen only if you're willing to do the hard work. (Get ready for the next chapter, which covers this!) You need to know who you are, what motivates you, and what value you bring. After all, this isn't just a job we're talking about. It's your future. ●

KNOW YOURSELF

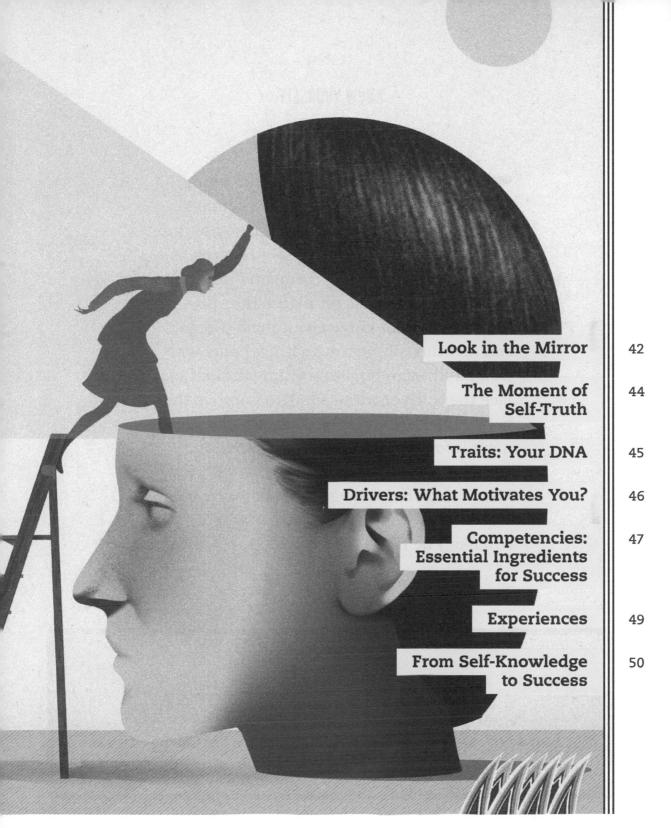

TWO

KNOW YOURSELF

Most people don't like being assessed. It makes them feel vulnerable. They make assumptions about their strengths (usually overestimating them) and underplay their weaknesses. As for their blind spots, they'd rather not know about them. Doctors run into this all the time with patients who would rather pretend everything is fine than face the truth about needing to improve their health. In the same way, in-depth assessment information can help you monitor and improve the health of your career by identifying your strengths, pinpointing your weaknesses, and helping you see where you will likely be more successful.

The Unspoken Truth

✖

Most people would rather avoid the truth than face it—even when that means missing out on opportunities to improve themselves.

When companies get into the assessment game, there's a natural tendency to feel that this is mighty intrusive. *What right,* you might wonder, *does a prospective or current employer have to ask me to take tests that seem to pry into everything except my love life?* Yes, you're asked a lot of questions about yourself, but the company is trying to determine your mindset, skills, and experience for a job that it, after all, is paying for with stockholders' funds. As we've already discussed, companies are under more pressure today than ever to hire as diligently as possible.

Yet even the most experienced senior executives don't seem to get this, and in missing the point, they put their entire careers in peril. Jeffrey was no exception. He spent most of his career at one company, rising through the ranks mostly because of seniority. As chief financial officer, he thought of himself as the heir apparent who would take over when the current CEO retired. Certainly, a lot of folks viewed it that way. Though the CEO's retirement was still a couple of years away, Jeffrey found himself sitting in the boss's office some days, thinking about how he might, well, change the art that was hanging on the walls.

But he was in for a surprise. The company's board of directors had beefed up succession planning over the past eighteen months to ensure that the right people were being placed into the right jobs. The succession-planning process also included assessments to identify employees' hidden strengths and uncover blind spots. With their strengths and weaknesses identified, they could be better developed and pre-

pared to take on senior leadership positions with broader responsibility. In addition, the board had been introduced to Korn Ferry's assessment tools that can distinguish best-in-class executive talent, and the directors wanted to ensure they identified the best candidates for the CEO role.

Jeffrey, however, resisted. Every time he was contacted by HR to arrange for his assessment, he blew it off with the usual excuses: too busy, traveling, end of the quarter, board meetings. Clearly, he put no value in the assessment process. His attitude was, *I'm the CFO, and the next step for me is becoming CEO.*  *Everybody in the company knows this. Why do I need to be assessed for the obvious?*

What Jeffrey didn't realize was that the board wanted him to be assessed. Some directors had expressed concerns about his readiness and ability to step into the top spot. The more Jeffrey delayed the assessment, the more suspicion he aroused as to why he was resisting. Finally, he couldn't stall any longer. He was brought in for a day of assessment exercises. The Korn Ferry consultants administering the tests could feel his hostility. Nothing they said or did seemed to help Jeffrey relax and embrace the process.

Needless to say, Jeffrey did not do well. The assessment uncovered some serious blind spots involving his ability to motivate and manage others. When the consultants presented the feedback to Jeffrey, framing it as an opportunity for him to further his development and build his leadership capabilities, he resisted that as well. He believed something must have been wrong with the assessment. He was off that day, not feeling his best, because he was much better than the assessment indicated.

The board found Jeffrey's assessment to be very informative. For many directors, it confirmed their suspicions that Jeffrey was not ready to become CEO. His negative attitude about being assessed and his unwillingness to address his blind spots only supported their doubts. When the CEO retired, Jeffrey did not get the job. Soon thereafter, he left the company, packing up the corner-office design brochures he'd quietly acquired.

Jeffrey's outcome potentially could have been very different had he embraced the assessment process and used the feedback to inform a development plan. No one is expected to score "100 percent"—everyone has strengths and weaknesses. Jeffrey's stubbornness and ego, however, undermined his chances of developing into a more capable leader and being named CEO.

As I mentioned, you'd be amazed at how detailed the recruiting and consulting industry has become at predicting and developing the skills top executives must have in particular fields. Our Korn Ferry Institute has probed through thousands of job-candidate profiles and identified the distinguishing characteristics possessed by the most sought-after talent.

Most Desirable Traits in Tomorrow's Talent

Highly skilled in engaging and inspiring others

Manages ambiguity (which is very common in today's fast-paced and ever-changing business environment) and has global perspective

Has strategic vision and the ability to align execution—meaning planning and prioritizing to further organizational goals

Comfortable taking risks and highly adaptable

Adept at influencing others and motivated by challenge

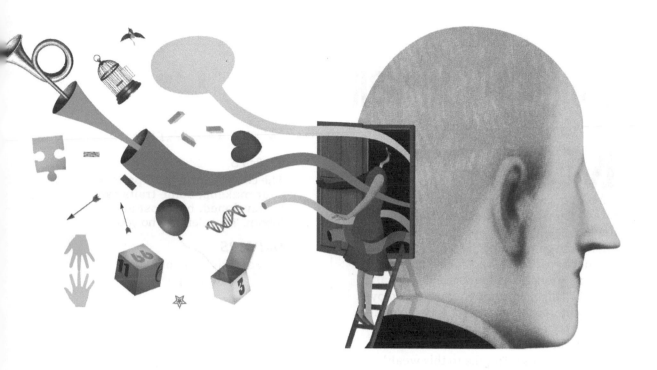

The most desirable traits can vary from one industry to another—from advanced technology to consumer goods, for instance—and from one position to another. An example I like to use involves financial services. The highest-ranked trait for top-grade middle managers is "courage," which makes sense, because we want the people in these roles to have the guts to find investments that will grow our money. But for this field's C-suite crowd, courage isn't as important as the ability to persuade and deal with all the ambiguity that unpredictable markets bring.

Clearly, knowing what characteristics (we break these down into competencies, traits, and drivers) matter in the field of your job hunt can give you a great edge. But you'll gain an objective view of yourself—your strengths and weaknesses, preferences and motivations—only if you are open to assessments and the knowledge they provide. It takes self-knowledge to engage in self-improvement.

And face it, you are going to be assessed at some point, whether in your current job or the next one. Even at the middle-management level, you'll find that employers want to know as much about you as possible: your strengths and weaknesses, your leadership style, how well you fit the culture, and so forth. You may not be formally assessed in a job interview, but you will be asked to identify and discuss your strengths and weaknesses. You can't fake these answers. You need to know yourself. To do that, you need to take a good, hard look in the mirror. ●

LOOK IN THE MIRROR

Most people want to skip this step. They want to launch directly into the job search. Their focus is 100 percent outward, looking for job opportunities. They spend little if any time looking inward. The truth is you must be self-aware enough to gain perspective about yourself. You need to identify and speak to your skills and experiences, what motivates you, and what all this means for your next employer.

Fortunately, there are tools that can help. Korn Ferry has decades of research and data about executives and what accounts for their success. Thanks to this wealth of intellectual property, we know executives better than they know themselves. Our IP, based on tens of millions of assessments of professionals and top executives, comes together in Korn Ferry's Four Dimensions of Leadership and Talent, or KF4D for short. This is what we use to assess executives for their strengths and weaknesses and to determine the kind of environment in which they'll most likely succeed.

In this book (and on our website, *www.KFAdvance.com/losetheresume*), we've adapted our IP into mini-assessments and exercises that will give you the insights you need in your job search. Although they are not as comprehensive as the long assessments we use for senior talent, you can still gain insights into yourself, to help you identify and articulate the value you bring and where you'll fit best in your next job. •

Who You Are

TRAITS
The core, "hard-wired" parts of your makeup. Some traits can be developed, but most are inborn. They define who you are.

DRIVERS
What motivates you; your passion and purpose.

What You Do

COMPETENCIES
The skills and abilities you have that are essential to success.

EXPERIENCES
The story you tell based on what you've accomplished.

TRAITS

↓

Inclinations, aptitudes, and natural tendencies a person leans toward, including personality traits and intellectual capacity.

For Example

Assertiveness, risk taking, confidence, and aptitude for logic and reasoning.

DRIVERS

↓

Values and interests that influence a person's career path, motivation, and engagement.

For Example

Power, status, autonomy, and challenge.

KF4D ASSESSES FOUR AREAS

COMPETENCIES

↓

Skills and behaviors required for success that can be observed.

For Example

Decision quality, strategic mindset, global perspective, and business insight.

EXPERIENCES

↓

Assignments or roles that prepare a person for future opportunities.

For Example

Functional experiences, international assignments, turnarounds, and fix-its.

THE MOMENT OF SELF-TRUTH

Let's be honest: A good portion of you probably looked at the graphic on the previous page and decided you're going to skip or skim the next few pages—and our tests in the Appendix—because you're convinced that you don't need to know anything about your traits, drivers, competencies, and experiences. You want to get to the "good stuff"—how to get a job. Big mistake.

If you're looking for what you've been missing in your career all along—what has prevented you from progressing on a career path with increasingly meaningful positions—this is it. These are assessments given to CEOs and other C-suite executives in leading global organizations. It's giving you what they have had all along. As the saying goes (or as I think I heard in a yoga class I passed by): Claim your strengths and make friends with your weaknesses. •

SOCRATES

KNOW THYSELF

I'm a great thinker. No, I'm faking my intelligence. People love to hear my voice at work. No, they make excuses to get coffee when I approach. If you're like most people, your opinion of yourself and your work is frenetic. Or it stays the same—and is totally wrong! How you see yourself usually bears little relation to how colleagues do. Research shows that when rating someone, bosses, peers, direct reports, and customers agreed with each other's assessments more than with the way the person rated himself or herself. So if you want to know more about yourself, you need feedback from another source.

TRAITS: YOUR DNA

Are you an optimist? Are you curious? Do you relate easily to others? These are examples of traits that exert a strong influence on your behavior.

Think of your traits as your natural tendencies and abilities. They include your personality traits and intellectual capacity. Traits guide your behavior, but at times they can be difficult to observe, which is why assessments are so important. Although traits are part of "who you are," they can change slowly over time as you take on new challenges. For example, with practice and even some coaching, an introvert can become more outgoing and comfortable speaking with others.

Traits not only affect how you perform in your current job, they also determine your future.

Here are some common traits and how they are defined in a business context. When you're ready (and don't put this off), you can flip to our Appendix to do a test and score yourself on your traits.

ADAPTABILITY Comfortable with unanticipated changes of direction or approach. Those who are highly adaptable are willing and able to nimbly change, adapt easily to changes in situations, adjust to constraints, and manage or rebound from adversity.

ASSERTIVENESS Able to take charge and direct others. People who are assertive tend to be seen as aggressive and decisive.

CURIOSITY Can tackle problems in a novel way, sees patterns in complex information, and pursues deep understanding. Those who are very curious enjoy solving complex problems with creative solutions and addressing issues in thoughtful and intellectually driven ways.

FOCUS Has a preference for organization, procedure, and exactitude. Those who are highly focused demand structure and tend to be seen as systematic, detail-oriented, and in control.

NEED FOR ACHIEVEMENT Motivated by work or activities that allow your skills and abilities to be tested against external standards. Those with a high need for achievement appreciate working hard, judge their own achievements according to their goals, and strive to meet and exceed standards.

PERSISTENCE Passionate and steadfast in pursuit of personally valued long-term or lifetime goals, despite obstacles, discouragement, or distraction. Highly persistent people push through obstacles and do not give up on difficult tasks.

RISK TAKING Willing to take a risk or a stand. Those who are comfortable with risk taking may prefer success over security and exhibit a willingness to take substantial risk when making decisions.

TOLERANCE OF AMBIGUITY Comfortable with uncertain, vague, or contradictory information. People who can handle ambiguity are energized by these situations, are open to alternative solutions, and can work productively despite not having a clear view of the future. ●

DRIVERS: WHAT MOTIVATES YOU?

What drives you? What preferences, values, and motivations influence your career choices? Your drivers are determined by who you are and by the circumstances or context at any given time.

Your drivers or motivators lie at the heart of critical questions: What's most important to you? What do you find rewarding? Most significant, your drivers factor into culture fit, engagement, and performance.

Drivers can be very specific or broad. They also can fluctuate based on your circumstances or stage in life. At every stage, they are crucial to where you will fit best—in what kind of company culture and environment, and working for what kind of boss—and how likely you are to be engaged by your job.

When you know what drives you, it is easier to find an organization that is aligned with your purpose. In the same way, when organizations understand what drives people, they find it easier to connect with them—to understand what makes them tick and tap into their energy. If there's a mismatch between a person's drivers and the organizational culture, that's bad news for all involved.

Here are some drivers and how they affect motivation and performance in the workplace. (Again, be sure to take our tests in the Appendix.)

COMPETENCIES: ESSENTIAL INGREDIENTS FOR SUCCESS

What makes you successful? It's a straightforward question that most people can't answer. They fumble around, describing what they've done. But they have no idea what their competencies are, because they don't understand the concept.

BALANCE The motivation to achieve balance between work and personal life. Those who score high in this area prefer work-related flexibility and broadly defined self-development, and they avoid high-stress, life-defining job roles.

CHALLENGE The motivation to achieve in the face of tough obstacles. Those with this motivation prefer challenging and competitive work assignments and environments that often preclude them from operating comfortably and in familiar ways.

COLLABORATION The preference to work interdependently, to make decisions and pursue goals in a group. Those who are highly collaborative prefer to be part of teams, to build consensus, share responsibility, and use social behaviors to achieve work-related success.

INDEPENDENCE The preference for independence and an entrepreneurial approach. Those who desire independence prefer freedom from organizational constraints and want to set and pursue their own vision. They also value employability over job security.

POWER The desire to achieve work-related status and influence, and to make an impact on the organization. Those who seek power desire higher levels of visibility and responsibility within an organization, and they want to acquire a high degree of influence.

STRUCTURE The preference for work-related stability, predictability, and structure. Those with this preference value job security, familiar problems and solutions, and jobs that often require depth and specialized knowledge or skill. •

Functional and technical skills are also part of your competencies. For example, if you're in finance, then having strong financial acumen is a big part of your competency.

Your competencies may include some natural talent. But many competencies are intentionally developed over time and built up as part of a particular job assignment. Some are harder to develop than others, but with the right motivation and support (coaching, stretch assignments, feedback) nearly everyone can make measurable progress on competencies.

Your competencies are how you drive results— the essential ingredients of your success. These are observable skills and behaviors, such as resourcefulness, courage, or decision making.

Here are some competencies, grouped by category according to how they can help you achieve results and realize success. (Don't forget to test yourself in the Appendix.)

Thought

BALANCES STAKEHOLDERS Anticipating and balancing the needs of multiple stakeholders.

CULTIVATES INNOVATION Creating new and better ways for the organization to be successful.

GLOBAL PERSPECTIVE Taking a broad view when approaching issues; using a global lens.

STRATEGIC VISION Seeing ahead to future possibilities and translating them into breakthrough strategies.

Results

ALIGNS EXECUTION Planning and prioritizing work to meet commitments aligned with organizational goals.

ENSURES ACCOUNTABILITY Holding yourself and others accountable for meeting commitments.

People

DEVELOPS TALENT Developing people to meet their career goals and the organization's goals.

ENGAGES AND INSPIRES Creating a climate in which people are motivated to do their best to help the organization achieve its objectives.

MANAGES CONFLICT Handling conflict situations effectively and with a minimum of noise.

NAVIGATES NETWORKS Effectively building formal and informal relationships inside and outside the organization.

PERSUADES Using compelling arguments to gain the support and commitment of others.

Self

COURAGE Stepping up to address difficult issues; saying what needs to be said.

MANAGES AMBIGUITY Operating effectively, even when things are not certain or the way forward is not clear.

NIMBLE LEARNING Actively learning through experimentation when tackling new problems; using both successes and failures as learning fodder.

SITUATIONAL ADAPTABILITY Adapting approach and demeanor in real time to match shifting demands of different situations. •

EXPERIENCES

There's no surprise about experiences. They're what you've done.

Your experiences are defined by the roles and assignments that make up your career history—the bullet points on your resume. What most people don't fully appreciate, though, is what experiences are meant to do.

Experiences transcend job titles. Whether someone is a front-line manager or a senior vice president is less relevant than what he or she has accomplished. Experiences are not a grocery list of what you've done. They provide keen insights into what you've accomplished and how these accomplishments can be applied to your next employer.

Your experiences are meant to be a summary of your progression that allows people to get to know you. This isn't supposed to be an exhaustive list—which is what a client named Bert thought. I'll admit that Bert had amazing leadership experiences in the military and the business world. But when I asked him to tell me about himself, it became a long, one-sided conversation. He launched into a discussion of his experiences *in great detail*—a long litany of everything he had done. For thirty-six minutes (I surreptitiously timed it) Bert talked *at me*. This was not a meaningful discussion of experiences; it was a filibuster.

Amassing experiences is akin to strength training at the gym: The weight and repetitions both matter. Heavyweight jobs are those that include high visibility, a risk of failure, ambiguity, and a broad scope of responsibility. The more difficult and perspective-broadening the experience, the faster it bulks up leadership muscle. But depth of experience matters for leaders and leaders-in-training. •

Your experiences should tell a story about you and your career progression from one position to the next.

FROM SELF-KNOWLEDGE TO SUCCESS

When you're committed to learning more about yourself, you understand your strengths and can communicate them more clearly and meaningfully to a prospective employer, just as you'll identify your weaknesses and be able to address your blind spots. Looking at the truth and learning about yourself is the secret to success.

Make no mistake, most self-explorations are not much fun and definitely require the right attitude. But when I think of people who were willing to give this a shot, I'm reminded of some amazing success stories.

Some years ago, for example, Pamela was the chief marketing officer of a retail chain and among the half-dozen candidates from across the company being groomed to possibly take over the CEO position within the next five years. No one was the hands-down favorite. While Pamela had definite strengths, particularly involving strategy and motivating people, she also had blind spots—and she knew it. So when the company wanted the leading succession candidates to be assessed against the requirements of the CEO position, Pamela embraced the process.

The feedback was hard-hitting to be sure. Being highly self-aware, Pamela knew she had weaknesses in certain areas, such as financial acumen. The assessment, though, showed additional blind spots, revealing that she needed to work intensely on developing a global perspective, engaging and inspiring others, and tolerating ambiguity. Pamela took it all in, knowing that if she wanted to advance in her career she needed to close these gaps. Without the assessment, she couldn't possibly be prepared.

The day after she received the feedback, Pamela emailed the Korn Ferry assessment team. "I'm back in the office today, and I'm already working on my development areas," she wrote. Sure, it may sound a little Pollyannaish, but she took steps immediately. She convened her direct reports to share what she had learned about herself. Within a week, she had a plan to get three stretch assignments from the CEO, and she was seeking bi-monthly feedback. To solidify her commitment, she hired a coach to work with her. Today, she is the CEO of a Fortune 1000 company.

But don't mistake the end for the moral of this story. It's not about having the best assessment. What matters most is what you do with the assessment information. As many CEOs will tell you, it's better to have someone who didn't assess well initially but accepted feedback and got better than someone who did well at first and didn't improve.

Hunger to improve wins. If you combine that hunger with passion and purpose, you will have an amazing career journey—wherever it takes you. •

BE A LEARN-IT-ALL

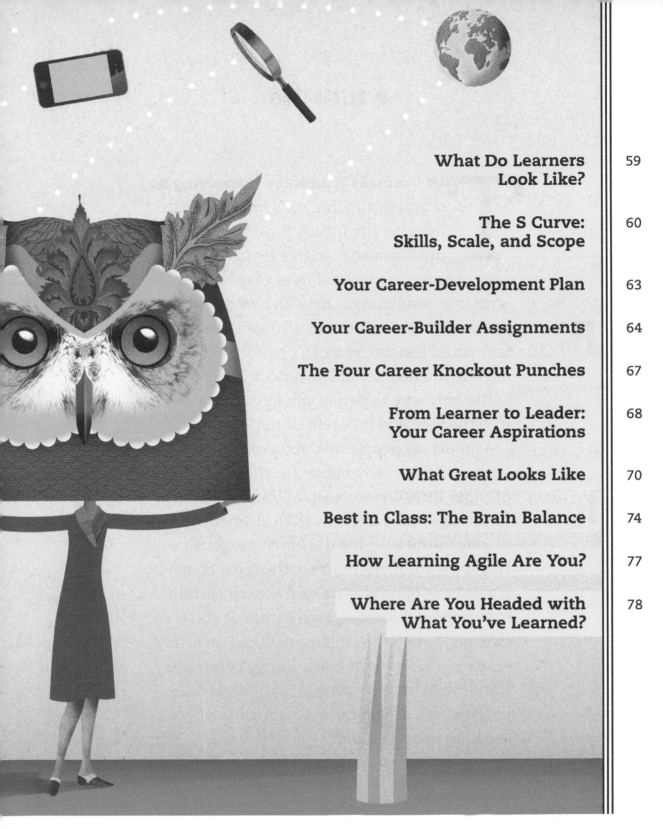

BE A LEARN-IT-ALL

The business landscape is evolving so dramatically that's it's impossible to imagine the future. Big data, artificial intelligence, machine learning, and a host of emerging technologies may be only the start of a revolution in how and where work is performed. In the face of such unpredictable, fast-paced change, you can't possibly know it all. But you had better learn it all! Learning is the only way to parlay what you know now into the new and different of tomorrow.

As much as people talk about being "lifelong learners," few really make the effort. It's one of those little fibs we keep telling ourselves or saying at job interviews: No, it's not the money or the title; it's the *learning experience* that we want more than anything. Of course, it's just the opposite. You are almost certain to ask about a company's vacation or start-date policy before you inquire about its last employee-training session. Rarely is anyone thinking, *What am I going to learn in this new position?* Yet, as you pursue your career path, learning matters most.

LEARNING OUTSIDE THE CLASSROOM

Research shows that development occurs mostly through opportunities, such as stretch assignments.

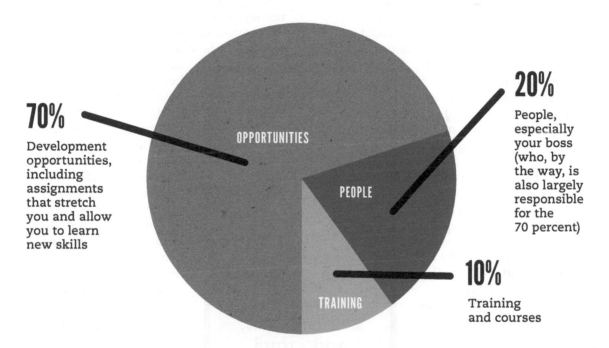

70%
Development opportunities, including assignments that stretch you and allow you to learn new skills

OPPORTUNITIES

PEOPLE

TRAINING

20%
People, especially your boss (who, by the way, is also largely responsible for the 70 percent)

10%
Training and courses

You may need a little convincing before you buy into this idea of the value of learning, but here are the brutal facts: The average number of years spent in a job today is about four, and for those under the age of thirty-five, it's between two and three years (and even less for younger workers). That's a lot of career movement. So much, in fact, that you'd better make it meaningful. Back in the day, when people stayed put at one big company, there were many ways to advance and earn more money at one place. But with all the hopping, skipping, and jumping going on today, Korn Ferry research shows learning is the number-one determinant of a person's earnings for life. It only makes sense with every job to focus on the learning opportunities, so that you're better positioned for the next move and the one after that.

Early on in my career I was told "be known for something"—and be indispensable to someone. I didn't listen to every piece of advice from my mentors, but this one sunk in. It changed my attitude toward learning, and my career trajectory. In every job, I sought to learn all I could and challenged myself to know something that no one else (or few others) knew. My objective was not to be a know-it-all, but rather a learn-it-all. As a result, I believe, my engagement took a quantum leap.

Let's be real about this: Immediate needs are important, including making more money. We've all been there. When I give a speech, I usually ask for a show of hands from audience members who think they are overpaid and from ones who think they are underpaid. Almost always, every hand goes up when I ask about being underpaid. Rarely is a hand raised when I ask about being overpaid. It's understandable that you want to make more money, so you give salary oversized importance. But you can't take a job only because it pays more and not think about what it will do for your career trajectory. You have to consider what you will learn in that job to better position yourself for the future.

The danger is being blinded by "the bling" of the salary and ignoring the real opportunities. Bryan was a teacher who was well liked by colleagues and respected by parents and students, but he was fed up with his salary. As he saw it, so many other people were making much more money, why shouldn't he? The opportunity that caught Bryan's eye was mortgage lending. This was the early 2000s, when the housing market was heating up in the years preceding the financial crisis of 2008 and 2009.

Through mutual connections, Bryan reached out to me. We traded emails and met for coffee. "I can't believe all these people are making this kind of money," he told me. "How hard can it be to write loans all day? Anybody can do that."

I cautioned him against making the move, knowing he was making a big mistake. It was clear he had lost perspective, as many people do when it comes to how others make money. They think something is easy, when in fact it's very difficult. The mortgage-lending business, particularly in those days, was all about having a network of potential clients. Bryan assumed he could easily parlay his connections with other teachers and parents into a client base. In addition, he was counting on the mortgage company to provide support and training and to help him develop his client base.

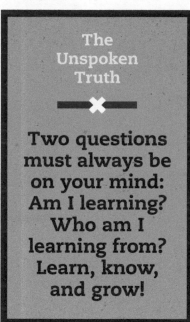

The Unspoken Truth

Two questions must always be on your mind: Am I learning? Who am I learning from? Learn, know, and grow!

Korn Ferry research shows learning is the number-one determinant of a person's earnings for life.

So Bryan gave up his full-time teaching job, along with the benefits and security, for what he saw as the "big-money" potential of earning commissions on the loans he wrote. Then reality hit: The mortgage company provided no help. Its recruitment policy—unfortunately, all too common—was to bring in people from varied backgrounds and see who "sticks." Companies that operate like this have a high turnover rate, but the few high performers they do bring in more than make up for the personnel losses along the way.

Within the first few months, Bryan knew he'd made a terrible mistake. His financial losses were considerable, and the stress on his marriage caused him and his wife to divorce. Currently, Bryan is working part-time as a teacher and trying to find a full-time position.

Of course, Bryan's tale is particularly rough. But it's another lesson about how you can't be shortsighted in your job search. You need to think and act in the context of your overall career path. The decisions you make today will affect where you will end up tomorrow. And there is no greater impact on your future than what you learn and the skills you develop. •

Learn It or Leave It Checklist

Is my work meaningful?

Am I engaged in what I am doing?
Does the organization I work for have
a mission/vision/purpose that I can
support and feel aligned with?

Who am I working for?

Am I working for a boss who champions
me, who wants to help me grow and
develop with challenging assignments?

Am I learning?

What new skills am I gaining?
While it's impossible to predict the
skills that will be needed in the future,
one thing is certain: If you don't learn,
you won't grow, and if you don't grow,
you'll never progress.

WHAT DO LEARNERS LOOK LIKE?

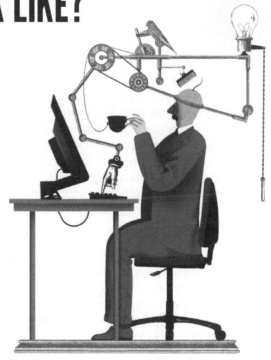

To be skilled at anything requires some knowledge and know-how. But more than that, you must possess the ability to adjust, adapt, and respond. In short, you need to learn. People who are curious and risk-takers are often the best learners. But learning doesn't follow the smooth road. Unless you have challenging job tasks in which you must perform and face the real risk of failing, you will not develop significantly. This is the essence of learning from experience so that you get better and succeed. This learning attitude brings into focus some more unusual skills.

Unless you face the real risk of failing, you will not develop significantly.

LEARNERS ARE WILLING TO FEEL AND LOOK STUPID

This is the only way to learn and perform well in new situations. Admit you don't know what to do and hit it with everything you've got. Not only are you soaking up information to expand your knowledge and skill base, but you are also learning how to contribute. You know you're not an expert, but you want to develop an expertise and become known for something. The only way to do that is to become exposed to as many learning situations as possible, and to be open to looking and feeling "stupid" or "clueless" as you navigate the learning curve.

LEARNERS ARE WORLD-CLASS OBSERVERS—OF THEMSELVES, OTHERS, AND SITUATIONS

You know that "wise voice" we all have that sits on our shoulder and gives advice to us all the time? With learners, that voice is objective and dispassionate: *What's going on here? How are people reacting? Why? What's working? What isn't? Is there anything I can take away that is repeatable?* Learners try to make sense of things, and a great way to do this is with continuous self-reflection and questioning of the process.

LEARNERS KNOW MORE IS BETTER

Learners have more ways to handle situations because they have more conscious learning tactics. They will try anything. They'll keep a journal, write down a plan, or engage in a visioning exercise. In one study, effective supervisors had five times more methods for handling difficult employees than did the average supervisors. That's learning in action.

LEARNERS MAKE COMPARISONS

Learners will search the past for parallels, whether that means asking others in the company or reading a biography. They know there is nothing new, that history repeats itself, if only in broad themes.

LEARNERS MAKE SENSE THROUGH RULES OF THUMB

Many learners keep lists—mental or written—of things that might be true most of the time. These are guiding principles and trends they use to view situations.

LEARNERS ARE LIKELY TO HAVE A PLAN AND MEASURES OF SUCCESS AND FAILURE

Learners know what they are going to try and why, even if their plan is not written down. They evaluate what they did, decide what worked, and understand why it worked. Then they try again and again. The more tries, the more chances to learn to get it right. ●

THE S CURVE: SKILLS, SCALE, AND SCOPE

Most careers go through stages, each building upon the last. We might think of it as an S curve, like a road up a mountain. On the career path, those S's stand for *Skills, Scale,* and *Scope.*

First, you must increase your *skills* through a meaningful and logical career progression. Most of the job skills that matter for performance (such as strategy and planning) are learned on the job when people hit fresh challenges.

The jobs *most likely* to teach involve: starting something from nothing or almost nothing; fixing something that's broken; switching from a line role (involved in the company's core business) to a staff assignment (involved in support or specialized functions); and big changes in scope or scale, or taking on various kinds of projects.

The jobs *least likely* to teach are straight upward promotions, which often mean doing the same type of job again and again, and job

Where Learning Happens

Learning and development occur in the "first-time" and the "difficult." Comfortable circumstances in which you apply the skills you already have do not lead to growth. In fact, they often lead to stagnation. There's nothing like a good crisis for accelerating your learning.

switches aimed at gaining more exposure rather than taking on tough challenges.

In addition, you will need to show progress in *scale* and *scope*. Greater scale means jobs with an increase in "size"—a bigger budget, greater volume of business, managing more people, and overseeing more layers of the organization. Jobs with greater scope involve substantially more breadth, such as new or additional areas of business, increased visibility, and greater complexity. In addition, career progress should involve a sizable increase in the number of people managed or in the complexity of the people-related challenges faced.

These increases in skills, scale, and scope form the "stair-step" advancement that will be part of the "story you tell" to recruiters and hiring managers. Your career trajectory (or lack thereof) speaks volumes about you, your abilities and potential, your passion and commitment. That's why a lateral move can detract from your story. It's possible that you made one such move for a good reason. For example, you were in marketing and wanted greater exposure to operations. But two lateral moves will probably raise a red flag about why you were unable to advance into a position with greater responsibility. That's why you must use foresight as you plan for your next job, with the perspective of how you will continue to develop along your career trajectory. •

6 STAGES OF CAREER DEVELOPMENT
WHERE YOU LEARN, HOW YOU GROW

1
FOLLOWER
At the first phase, you are a follower. Typically, this is associated with a first professional job out of college. As a follower, you are action oriented and task focused as you carry out what others tell you to do. You will never lead if you don't know how to follow someone!

2
COLLABORATOR
Soon you will begin to collaborate with others. You're still operating from your technical skill set, but you begin to develop people skills through collaboration with peers on your team.

3
INSTRUCTOR
As a first-time team leader or manager, you're tapping your people skills when you give instructions to your team, which may comprise only one person. The key here is whether you effectively instruct people on what needs to be done, instead of being the one to do it. Jobs that help you progress at this level include:

STAFF LEADERSHIP
At this level, you have the responsibility but not the authority. Typical examples include planning projects, installing new systems, troubleshooting problems, negotiating with outside parties, and working in a staff group.

STAFF TO LINE SHIFTS
This involves moving to a job with an easily determined bottom line or results, managing bigger scope and/or scale, demonstrating new skills/perspectives, and taking on unfamiliar aspects of your assignments.

4
MANAGER
Your skill set builds as you manage larger teams with bigger goals and objectives. You will need to motivate direct reports and learn how to manage them by giving them objectives and goals, as well as the means to pursue and achieve them. For example, you may be in a "change-manager" role—managing a significant effort to change something or implement something of significance, such as total-work systems, business restructuring, major new systems and procedures, M&A integration, responses to major competitor initiatives, and reorganizations.

5
INFLUENCER
Now things get interesting! This stage is a transition away from directly managing a team to influencing people. Influence is a key leadership skill that you need to develop in order to work with people across the organization, especially those who do not report to you. In fact, you could be influencing people in other departments who are at your level, or even a level above you.

6
LEADER
At this level, you spend much of your time empowering and inspiring others. As a leader, you don't tell people what to do; rather, you tell them what to think about. Your biggest priority is to motivate people so that they can do more and become more than even they thought possible.

YOUR CAREER-DEVELOPMENT PLAN

With these insights, you can embark on a career-development plan as part of your job search. As with any long-term strategy, you'll need to look beyond the needs of the moment to consider a longer timeframe—especially the skill development you will need as you move from job to job. This will help you identify the jobs and assignments that will best increase your learning, expand your skills, and lead you to the next job.

CHOOSE WISELY

Figure out what is critically important to your performance in your next job or success in your career. Make sure that you're focused on something that matters to you and that other people think is important, as well. (This is what it means to be indispensable to someone else.) When you create your action plan, set a time frame. You will be more motivated and committed to your development when you see improvement.

GET SPECIFIC

Seek detailed feedback continuously. To discover your blind spots and find out more about what you need to develop, seek input from your mentors and others who know you well. Don't be defensive or try to rationalize. Tell them you are concerned about a specific need and require more information or feedback so you can focus on your growth and development as part of your career advancement. Be specific in your request. For example, if you just finished making a presentation, ask a peer or other colleague, "I have been working on my presentation skills. How well did I engage others?"

CREATE THE PLAN

Once you have input (from assessments or other sources) and feedback from others, you can create a plan. There are three kinds of action plans: what to stop doing, what to start doing, and what to keep doing. Getting ongoing, detailed feedback from others will help you see what you need to stop, start, and continue doing as you develop new competencies in your current and next positions.

LEARN FROM OTHERS

Look for role models, both on and off the job. What do these people do (and what don't they do) that makes them successful? Adopt the habits and behaviors that good role models exhibit.

TRY SOME STRETCHING TASKS

Seventy percent of skills development happens on the job. Your current or future position offers a great opportunity for your development. Brainstorm with your manager, mentor, or others about tasks and activities you can undertake to build specific skills and experience. Work on your areas of development. Start small with manageable tasks that can build your competence and confidence.

READ, STUDY, PRACTICE

There are numerous sources of information and inspiration about development, including how-to books, biographies/autobiographies, training courses, and development exercises. Put what you learn into practice and get feedback on your progress.

TRACK YOUR PROGRESS

Keeping track of your progress will keep you motivated and help you feel successful. The changes may be small, but over time you will make incremental progress that others will likely notice.

As an ongoing exercise, your career-development plan helps ground you in self-awareness and continuous improvement. Your focus is learning and growing, which become ingrained in everything you do, including looking for your next job. •

YOUR CAREER-BUILDER ASSIGNMENTS

Ideally, your career will follow a trajectory that includes bigger assignments, more responsibilities, and ample opportunities to stretch yourself. Along the way, you'll need intentional "career-builder" assignments to gain new skills and broader experiences that will be crucial later in your career. Seek out jobs providing specific experiences that allow you to develop and demonstrate capabilities, particularly in four key areas: having a global mindset, dealing with ambiguity, handling change, and mastering a faster pace. These areas of development are so important, in fact, weakness or absence of competencies in any of them could stall your career progression.

Achievements do not happen by magic or fate. In the same way, your career development will not result from some fortunate happenstance. It takes a deliberate approach. If you have your eye on a career trajectory that involves leading others one day—perhaps as a senior executive—you must possess "eight imperatives," which can be grouped into three major areas, as follows.

What You Do

1 Embrace **NEW EXPERIENCES** to spark learning and development.

2 Adopt **DELIBERATE PRACTICE AND REFLECTION** to build skills and automate changes.

3 **LEARN FROM OTHERS**, both in learning communities and when applying skills in the real world.

Who You Are

4 Leaders foster **A GROWTH MINDSET**; they have to care, and be curious and open.

5 Leverage **EMOTION** to spark motivation and activate effort.

6 Optimize **STRESS** to move out of a comfort zone and into a learning zone.

Pause

7 Practice **MINDFULNESS** to quiet ego and pause automaticity, creating space to choose a different approach.

8 Enact **BEHAVIORAL COMMITMENTS** to create a sustained personal change.

EIGHT CAREER-BUILDER IMPERATIVES

EMBRACING NEW EXPERIENCES highlights the importance of learning and development opportunities. Whether these experiences occur in the world, on the job, or in formal programs, they provide opportunities for enrichment, exploration, and engagement. Continuously responding to novel experiences also builds your capacity for agility.

ADOPTING DELIBERATE PRACTICE AND REFLECTION will help you acquire complex skills. Deliberate practice involves setting specific goals and making small changes in behavior based on feedback and monitoring your outcomes.

LEARNING FROM OTHERS reflects the 70-20-10 breakdown at the beginning of this chapter and the importance of learning through relationships. Having a mentor and/or a supportive boss who champions you will help you gain more learning.

FOSTERING A GROWTH MINDSET reminds you of the change that occurs only when you let go of what you followed/valued in the past and redefine yourself in some new ways. A growth mindset will help you overcome resistance to change and an "unconscious addiction" to the familiar.

LEVERAGING EMOTION speaks to the importance of emotion in helping you learn. As studies show, we don't remember just facts, but also the feelings associated with them. Emotion also facilitates development by fueling motivation. The more you understand your own emotions, the better you can recognize and understand others' emotions.

OPTIMIZING STRESS encourages you to move out of your comfort zone and into learning opportunities. Constructive stress can help you stretch and grow in response to challenges.

PRACTICING MINDFULNESS taps an inner state in which you can observe yourself in action. Instead of reacting automatically, you use mindfulness to create a "space" between a stimulus and your reaction. Mindfulness can empower you and allow you to assume greater responsibility in your life.

ENACTING BEHAVIORAL COMMITMENTS allows you to tap powerful drivers of personal change. Behavioral commitments set expectations for how you will act, react, and interact with others. With each commitment, you can change the dynamic in the moment and reinforce productive behavior.

By using these "eight imperatives" systematically, consistently, and in combination, you will increase your chances of creating and sustaining the kind of change that will increase your development and help secure your career trajectory. •

THE FOUR CAREER KNOCKOUT PUNCHES

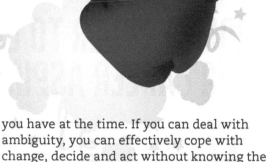

If your career aspirations include holding a leadership position at the higher level of an organization, you'll need experience in the four key areas outlined as follows. The omission of any one of them will be a "knockout punch" that will likely preclude you from moving into senior leadership.

1 GLOBAL

You will be required to show some global experience, such as an international assignment or, at a minimum, work on a global team that requires significant travel to operations or clients abroad. Such experiences are crucial for developing a *global mindset*, which every leader must possess to compete in a marketplace that is both borderless and heavily influenced by local nuance. You'll deal with different languages, cultural norms, and business rules, which will provide you with opportunities to grow and stretch. You'll develop cross-cultural agility, enabling you to work with and relate to people across multiple cultures.

2 DEALING WITH AMBIGUITY

You must be comfortable with ambiguity. In fact, studies show that 90 percent of the problems confronting middle managers and people in higher positions are ambiguous—neither the problem nor the solution is clear. Dealing with ambiguity means making good decisions based on the information you have at the time. If you can deal with ambiguity, you can effectively cope with change, decide and act without knowing the total picture, shift gears comfortably, and handle risk and uncertainty.

3 HANDLING AND MANAGING CHANGE

Organizations today are dealing with unprecedented levels of change. Consider the rapid advancements in technology: artificial intelligence and machine learning, the Internet of Things, and the disintermediation that continues to disrupt industries. Being comfortable with change means not only reacting to it, but also being a catalyst for it. You must demonstrate the ability to handle and manage change by putting new ideas into practice and being highly interested in continuous improvements. You are cool under pressure and can handle the heat and consequences of being on the front line of change.

4 MASTERING A FASTER PACE

Along with widespread change, businesses are experiencing a faster "pace of play." Everything from product cycles to time-to-market is being compressed, so you must be able to handle the faster pace. You know how to encourage others to work smarter and use technology to their advantage, but you don't push the organization at a pace faster than it can handle. •

FROM LEARNER TO LEADER: YOUR CAREER ASPIRATIONS

Whatever your aspirations, you must be true to yourself. Some people have their eye on the C-suite, preparing for it through much of their career. Their preparation can include the pursuit of advanced education such as an MBA. Others have no such ambition but want to develop deep expertise in a specific functional role or area. You have to know yourself and what you want.

Through my interactions with people over the years, I have found that the majority want to manage or lead others *in some capacity*. That may mean heading a team, department, division, or even an entire company. When it comes to leading others—even if it's a small team—you must understand one important aspect of career development: *What got you here won't take you there.*

I'm referring to your technical skills, or what I call "left-brain" skills. These are the "table stakes" of your current position. Of course, accountants must have expertise in accounting, just as teachers must know how to teach and computer programmers have to master coding. These left-brain technical skills are acquired through education and experience. But at some point, they matter less because that type of knowledge or expertise is assumed. As you try to advance in your career, people expect that

you have mastered the core requirements of your job. In other words, it's no surprise at a certain level that you excel at what you do functionally, but so does everyone else you're competing against for the next job or promotion: the accountant who wants to lead the finance team, the teacher who wants to become a principal, the computer programmer who wants to become the chief technology officer.

If you want to advance, you need to escape the "left-brain trap." You need to develop a complementary set of skills I call the "right brain." At the center of the right brain is the ability to connect with and influence others.

In every field or industry, leaders need a combination of left-brain technical expertise *and* right-brain mastery. The higher you rise, the more the right brain rules. These are the "social leadership" skills that enable a leader to interact with and relate to a diverse group of people. This means being able to engage and influence others and build relationships.

Now at this point in your career, you may be several rungs down the ladder from a leadership role. Perhaps you're just starting out in your career, or you're in middle management. All this talk of inspiring and motivating others seems distant and far removed from your position.

The fact is, from your first professional job out of college through your next positions and beyond, you need to pursue jobs and assignments in which you can develop a *full slate of holistic talents*—left-brain (technical) and right-brain (people skills). Otherwise, it will be very difficult for you to reach your career destination.

Devon was a talented engineer who managed several projects for his company. His engineering expertise and technical skill set were highly valued. But Devon's assessments showed he lacked core people skills. He wasn't good at displaying empathy and compassion, motivating a team, and communicating effectively. Without right-brain skills, Devon could not move beyond an engineering role.

Fortunately for Devon, his company wanted to invest in his development, and to his credit he was willing to engage in the hard work of becoming more self-aware. Assessment and development, along with coaching, gave Devon some basic right-brain competencies. But he would always need coaching and support on the people side to be effective in his career.

As this example shows, the left brain and right brain are not an "either/or" choice—it's an *and*. Your right-brain development is all about becoming a more rounded person and holistically prepared. If you want to progress beyond where you are now, you need to seek out jobs, assignments, and career opportunities that will allow you to grow and stretch you in both directions. •

Inspiring Others

One of the most important right-brain skills is the ability to inspire others—to motivate them to become their best selves and contribute to the fullest of their potentials. To inspire others, leaders must paint a compelling vision and convey an engaging message about a future that's fresh, exciting, and different from the present. The CEO isn't the only one who inspires. Leaders at every level—including the first-time manager who is leading a small team—can be inspiring. It takes honesty, authenticity, and genuine enthusiasm about the organization's mission and vision and the team's direct contribution to make that a reality.

WHAT GREAT LOOKS LIKE

As I mentioned, our researchers have spent years figuring out the skills and traits that have gotten people ahead. We've tried to take the guesswork out of identifying great leaders—and the intel couldn't be more useful for career planning. Drawing from assessments of nearly 30,000 people at the entry level, mid level, and C level, we compiled high-performance profiles that define what it takes to be great at each of these levels. In this section, you'll see how greatness is defined in two areas: how great leaders handle novel and uncertain situations (*Figure 1*) and how great leaders relate to or interact with others (*Figure 2*).

Figure 1 shows how the following key traits relate to performance in the context of handling novel and uncertain situations.

ADAPTABILITY
Being comfortable with unanticipated changes and diverse situations; being able to adjust to constraints and rebound from adversity.

CURIOSITY
Approaching problems in novel ways; seeing patterns and understanding how to synthesize complex information; having the desire to achieve deep understanding.

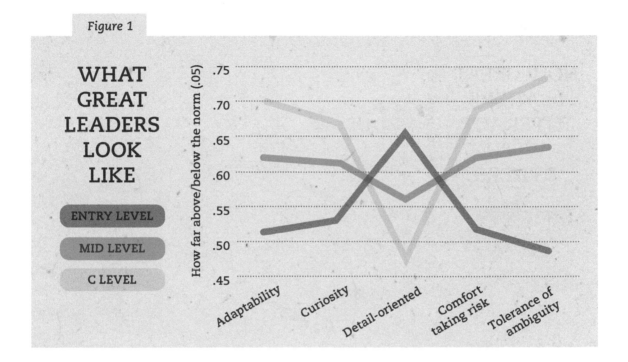

Figure 1

WHAT GREAT LEADERS LOOK LIKE

ENTRY LEVEL

MID LEVEL

C LEVEL

How far above/below the norm (.05)

Adaptability · Curiosity · Detail-oriented · Comfort taking risk · Tolerance of ambiguity

DETAIL-ORIENTED

Having the ability to systematically carry out tasks as assigned, with an understanding of the procedures and the importance of exactitude.

COMFORT TAKING RISK

Ability to take on and handle risk; higher-level positions typically involve more high-risk and high-profile situations.

TOLERANCE OF AMBIGUITY

Being comfortable with uncertainty and willing to make decisions and plans in the face of incomplete information.

Focusing on the center of the chart, we can see that being detail oriented is a trait that makes an entry-level person great. Here, the expectation is that employees will carry out their assigned tasks and responsibilities as instructed. The greater the focus on detail at the entry level, the more coworkers and bosses can count on assignments being completed thoroughly and accurately. In fact, detail orientation is so important, it is the "peak" for the high-performing entry-level employee.

For the middle manager and especially for the C-level leader, detail orientation appears less pronounced (a lower target to hit), but it remains an important aspect of being an effective leader. These executives are still concerned with the details, knowing that they can make or break any plan or strategy. However, at the mid level and

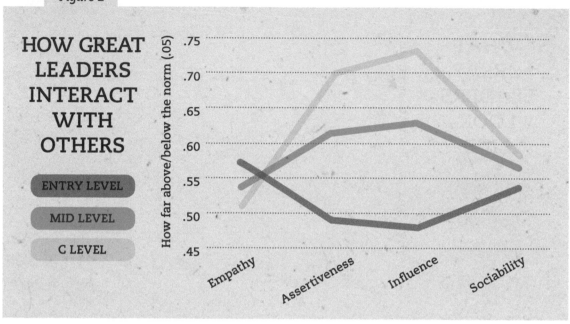

Figure 2

HOW GREAT LEADERS INTERACT WITH OTHERS

ENTRY LEVEL

MID LEVEL

C LEVEL

How far above/below the norm (.05)

.75 .70 .65 .60 .55 .50 .45

Empathy   Assertiveness   Influence   Sociability

especially at the C level, high performance means successfully delegating to others. A mid-level or senior leader who gets personally bogged down in the details, in fact, is ineffective and will not have the necessary mental bandwidth to focus on strategy.

From entry level to mid level, we see that excellence means ramping up in adaptability and tolerance of ambiguity, both of which come with experience, particularly involving decision making and taking on greater responsibility. These two traits are developed even further at the C level, where high-performing leaders must be extremely adaptable and highly tolerant of ambiguity so they not only react to change, but also initiate it.

Finally, at all three levels, curiosity is a distinguishing trait—and key to the upward

movement from entry level to mid level and eventually C level. For the high-performing entry-level person, curiosity goes beyond the normal learning curve and includes taking the initiative to soak up new experiences and build new skills. For mid-level managers who distinguish themselves, curiosity leads to competencies in new areas, such as taking on stretch assignments that are almost beyond their capabilities, or immersing themselves in the unfamiliar, such as working in a different country or region. For the C-level leader, curiosity prompts the engagement in lifelong learning, which is a prerequisite to greatness.

In *Figure 2*, we move to the emotional qualities that define high performance in how people interact with others.

Lifelong learning is a prerequisite to greatness.

EMPATHY

Having concern for and awareness of others' feelings, problems, and motivations.

ASSERTIVENESS

Enjoying taking charge and directing others; being decisive.

INFLUENCE

Motivating and persuading others; being adept at interpersonal relationships.

SOCIABILITY

Enjoying interactions with others; being energized by the presence of others and easily initiating social interactions.

As the chart shows, the entry-level person is the mirror opposite of the mid-level manager and the C-level executive in both assertiveness and influence. While some people are naturally more assertive than others, it is a quality that can be developed with time and experience. For example, you can take on assignments to lead projects and eventually, to lead people. Influence, not surprisingly, is a low point for the inexperienced entry-level person, but far more developed for the high-performing middle manager—and a key strength for great leaders. Highly adept C-level leaders leverage their influence and their network to align the team behind unifying goals and a sense of mission.

The two ends of the emotional spectrum as depicted here—empathy and sociability—show comparatively little difference at all levels. The high-performing entry-level person who must rely on others for coaching and mentoring is very focused on the needs of others—more so than mid-level and C-level leaders. Sociability is equal at the mid level and C level, given the need for these high-performing leaders to interact easily with others. But entry-level people who distinguish themselves are not far behind, displaying people skills that ingratiate them with others and enable them to interact with peers and with colleagues in positions several levels above their own.

As these profiles show, greatness is developed and displayed in a natural progression at every level. With greater awareness of the traits and qualities that define high performance at each level, you can amplify your strengths and develop your weaknesses. Coaching, mentoring, and assignments that will expand your capabilities in these areas will increase your chances of becoming a high performer. •

BEST IN CLASS: THE BRAIN BALANCE

While the final section of this chapter takes the long-term view of your career progression, don't lose sight of the very real application of these insights into your current job search. You need to demonstrate an array of abilities (left- and right-brain) to stand out from the crowd. Even if you haven't had much career development at this point, you need to demonstrate your potential. This way, an employer can hire you for a specific job today and develop you for positions in the future. (Once again, we see the importance of a boss who can provide you with opportunities to learn and grow.)

So what does "best in class" look like in terms of leadership? Given the millions of executive assessments we've conducted, we know what greatness looks like at the highest levels of organizations. Even if you never get there—and even if your aspirations don't take you in that direction—it's informative and inspiring to look at these traits and consider how they might apply in your current and future roles. Think of it in terms of developing your ability to play a sport. You may not ever be able to golf like Phil Mickelson or dunk a basketball like LeBron James, but by studying what they do, you can become a better player. At Korn Ferry, we think the same way about leadership at every level, from first-time managers all the way to the C-suite.

As our research shows, best-in-class CEOs have a balance of left-brain and right-brain skills. On the left-brain side, they have strengths in areas such as driving growth, strategic thinking, financial acumen, and managing in a crisis. Complementing these skills are a host of right-brain capabilities. Top of the list here are social and people skills that enable a leader to connect with, motivate, and inspire others. People skills enable leaders to have genuine compassion for others, to empathize and sympathize around work and non-work issues. Leaders who lack compassion will be seen as cold and uncaring, and will fail to motivate and

> Develop your right brain. In every interaction you have with people, they should feel better afterward than they did before.

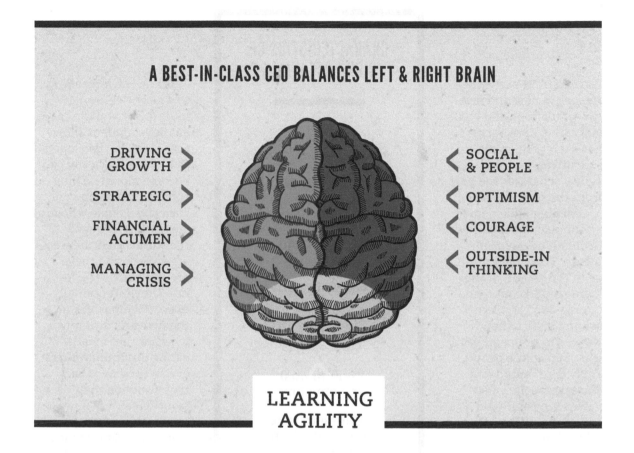

A BEST-IN-CLASS CEO BALANCES LEFT & RIGHT BRAIN

DRIVING GROWTH >

STRATEGIC >

FINANCIAL ACUMEN >

MANAGING CRISIS >

< SOCIAL & PEOPLE

< OPTIMISM

< COURAGE

< OUTSIDE-IN THINKING

LEARNING AGILITY

inspire others. Right-brain leadership also means exuding optimism to help others see there really is a way forward, even in difficult circumstances. Right-brain leaders are courageous. They know what needs to be said at the right time to the right person and in the right manner—especially when it's not positive. Courageous leaders speak up when others might be tempted to keep quiet, even if it means taking some heat.

In addition, best-in-class leaders exhibit "outside-in thinking" with a strong cus-tomer focus that helps them develop an almost intuitive sense of what new or improved products and services customers will want. They can gauge a plethora of external forces—including mega-trends, competitors, product innovation, and new markets—from customers' perspectives.

The foundation of left-brain and right-brain skills is one of the most important traits anyone can possess at any level: *learning agility*. Learning agility is defined as the willingness and ability to apply lessons learned from past experiences to new and first-time situations and challenges. As Korn Ferry has seen with countless executives, learning agility separates the best from the rest.

Learning-agile people are nimble and adaptable in changing environments. They don't just go to the default of the "same old" solution and "status quo" problem-solving tactics that worked in the past. With learning agility, people apply fresh approaches, ideas, and solutions.

Learning agility is one of the differentiating characteristics of a sought-after group of individuals: *high potentials*. These special talents are known for performing their jobs very well. They are competent, dependable, and reliable. They are motivated and willingly go the extra mile on any assignment. They are also *agile learners*—insatiably curious and engaged with the world around them.

Agile learners are willing to go against the grain of what they know how to do and prefer to do. Why? They are always seeking to get better and to learn new skills and ways of behaving.

CHARACTERISTICS OF HIGH-POTENTIALS

Easily learn new tasks and functions

Enjoy and deal well with ambiguity and complexity

Don't accept the status quo

Urgently impatient

Like to try new things, different approaches

Tend to push the envelope

Willing to take the heat when things fail

While learning agility, to a large degree, is inborn, our work in talent development shows that it can be developed. One of the ways you can become more learning agile is to develop your curiosity. People who are curious are engaged in the world. Their interests are varied, and they are constantly learning. They intentionally expose themselves to the new and different, whether that means eating unfamiliar foods or listening to music that's outside their favorite genre. They approach every day as a new opportunity to learn something, especially about themselves. That's why best-in-class CEOs begin and end the day with self-reflection.

People who want to become more learning agile seek out and embrace feedback and willingly take on challenging assignments. They learn from others, particularly those who are strong in areas where they are weak. They leverage the insights from bosses and mentors to gain a fuller view of where they are in their development and what they need to focus on next. Most of all, they know that learning never ends. •

HOW LEARNING AGILE ARE YOU?

To get an indication of how learning agile you are, take the following quiz. At the end, add up the points for each response and compare to the scoring grid.

1 POINT = STRONGLY DISAGREE
2 POINTS = DISAGREE
3 POINTS = AGREE

10–20 POINTS

Your pattern of scores indicates a predisposition toward "learning agility"— especially change agility and mental agility. The ability to deal with uncertainty and change, while having the capacity to tolerate a lack of details, is a hallmark of the agile approach to work.

21–30 POINTS

Your pattern of scores indicates a predisposition toward diligence and dutifulness. Detail orientation and a need for certainty are hallmarks of a strong contributing employee, but they can impede promotion and are in many ways the opposite of an agile approach to work.

[   ] IT'S IMPORTANT THAT I ATTEND TO EVERY DETAIL.

[   ] I ACCEPT NOTHING LESS THAN PERFECTION.

[   ] THE WORK ISN'T FINISHED UNTIL EVERY DETAIL HAS BEEN WORKED OUT WITH DUE DILIGENCE.

[   ] RULES ARE NOT MEANT TO BE BROKEN.

[   ] I WORK BEST WHEN GOALS AND SOLUTIONS ARE CLEAR.

[   ] STABILITY AND CLARITY ARE KEY TO A SUCCESSFUL CAREER.

[   ] FLEXIBILITY LEADS TO MISTAKES.

[   ] I ALWAYS STRIVE TO ACHIEVE CERTAINTY SO THAT WORK IS DONE CORRECTLY.

[   ] MAKING DECISIONS WITHOUT FULL INFORMATION IS BAD FOR THE COMPANY.

[   ] IT'S IMPORTANT TO ACHIEVE A STABLE AND RELIABLE WORK ENVIRONMENT.

WHERE ARE YOU HEADED WITH WHAT YOU'VE LEARNED?

The bottom line is pretty simple: Your career path is of your own making. From job to job, you create a trajectory that, ideally, should demonstrate increasing mastery, with bigger responsibilities and more demanding assignments. This does not happen by chance. It is part of a deliberate plan that begins right now, with your next job. Driving that progression is lifelong learning—authentic, targeted, and continual.

The more you learn and grow, the more chances you will have for success (and to make more money). Learning becomes the means *and* the end, because even if you reach the ultimate objective of your career trajectory, you should always be learning. •

TARGETING YOUR NEXT OPPORTUNITY

FOUR

TARGETING YOUR NEXT OPPORTUNITY

You could excuse Jed for thinking that he was above all this effort—this "job-hunting stuff," as he liked to say. Jed was a college friend who had spent most of his career at one of the big-name companies that always seem to make the cover of *Fortune*. As senior vice president, he wasn't quite in the C-suite, but he'd had enough one-on-one lunches with current and future company leaders and had worn tuxedoes to enough company-sponsored events to know he had a place in the firm for life.

The problem was that over the two decades he was at his *Fortune*-cover company, its life span was shortening, in a very gradual, painful way. Competition, globalization, technology—you name it—had left his job half the size it used to be. Along with Jed's job, something else was receding: his hairline. Nervous that the jig soon would be up, he started quietly crafting his LinkedIn profile with an absurd obsession about the merits of one phrase over another, such as "headed up a department" versus "ran" it. He also began endorsing his LinkedIn connections, hoping they would do the same for him. All this effort made him think online polishing was all he needed to do. Heck, at last count he had a *whopping* 312 connections. (Yes, I'm being sarcastic.) He kept telling himself that surely *someone out there* would recognize his talent. *Someone!*

And of course, we know how this turned out. The company was bought, and Jed discovered that there were no great eyeballs in the sky focused on him—and only him. In fact, he was dismayed at how empty his email inbox became. That "messy" job-hunting work would have to start, and hopefully it wasn't too late.

Certain job skills will always be in great demand. Technology creates demands out of nowhere. For example, the three big U.S. auto firms are spending billions of dollars trying to hire and pay every software expert they can find to design the perfect driverless car. But unless you catch lightning in a bottle or have managed to create an unusual buzz about yourself (perhaps with frequent TV news appearances), nobody is going to come looking for you. Indeed, it's incredibly humbling to discover how much talent—at all levels—is in such ridiculous supply.

The Unspoken Truth

People do more research when buying a flat-screen TV or a washing machine than when they're looking for a job.

So you need to seek out the job you want, and that's going to mean everything from taking a brand-new approach to networking to avoiding the "12 deadly sins" of interviewing. But the step that everyone seems to skip is *targeting your next opportunity.* That's a shame, because it's a great way to reduce your odds of putting a limited resource—your time—into efforts that make no sense.

Whether that opportunity exists at this moment is irrelevant; you create the opportunity. The objective is to match who you are—your "KF4D" of the traits, drivers, and competencies you identified in Chapter Two—with the roles to which you are most suited within the companies where you'd be a great fit. Some of this—such as asking where you want to live—may sound basic, but you would be amazed at how many people mess it up. Then there's the detective work on specific industries and companies that you can do with mind-blowing detail. You are looking for that intersection where your purpose and the company's purpose align, in an environment where you can thrive. That's where you'll find meaning in your work, and naturally boost your motivation and your performance in a role that's best suited to you.

Equally important, the more you target your desired opportunities, the easier it will be for people in your network to help you. If you're not clear about what you want, people can't engage with you in the process. You have to help them help you!

Ironically, when we were younger, we intuitively knew how targeting worked. I was reminded of this recently when I took my kids to an ice cream shop. Sitting at a table in the corner was a teenager filling out a job application. Did that take me back to my high school days! Back then, you'd go to the place you wanted to work and ask if they were hiring. If the manager or owner wasn't busy, you'd get an "interview" on the spot. And if your buddies worked there, they'd put in a good word for you. In fact, you probably found out about the job from a friend, who provided a "warm introduction" to the manager for you.

But as our careers progressed, we got the idea that we must wait for the job to come to us—or that we can be passive about it by sending out resumes online. The Internet is partially responsible. In one social-media platform after another, we're told how many "followers" or "connections" we have, but we're never given any context on how insignificant those numbers really are. Everyone is a big shot—in his or her own tiny world, and that world may have nothing to do with the next job. So the process we understood so well as teenagers—and that worked so well in those days—has begun to elude us. We forgot that the same fundamental rules apply: know where you want to go and then get a warm introduction. Even at the senior-most level,

it's not that different from the ice cream shop.

People are confounded by the job-search process. Some are genuinely confused about how to make things happen for themselves. Others don't want to do the necessary hard work. But there's no avoiding it. You've got to do the legwork. Korn Ferry's career coaches, working with individuals who are becoming proactive in managing their careers, teach targeting tactics to job seekers. (Visit our site *www .KFAdvance.com*.) These coaches advise and guide, but they don't do the hard work. That's up to the job seeker, who must be fully engaged in the targeting process. ●

IT'S ALL ABOUT YOUR EFFORT

The fact is, people do more research when buying a flat-screen TV or a washing machine than when they're looking for a job. For a major appliance or a new car, they'll spend hours online, comparing one brand's features to another and reading dozens of customer reviews. They will talk to friends about their recommendations and experiences. When buying a car, they will insist on taking test drives. But ask them what company culture suits them best, or what kind of boss they want to work for, and they have no idea. It's a common problem at all levels. People know they want a job, but they don't really know where or how to look.

Such was the case with Alicia, a very successful executive who had worked for some top companies. She reached out to speak with me through a mutual connection, and we met for coffee. I expected her to have some specific companies in mind and to want to talk about getting introductions to them.

Instead, Alicia looked at me and said, "I want to get a new job. Any suggestions?"

I couldn't believe it! Despite her impressive career path and seven-figure compensation, Alicia had fewer ideas of where she wanted to go than my college-age children and their friends do. All she knew was, because of family obligations, she wanted to be in the San Francisco area, but she could conceivably work anywhere in California.

"Start there," I told Alicia. "Identify the companies in the city where you want to live, then figure out the ones that have the culture you best align with."

This isn't rocket science, folks. But it seemed like news to Alicia. Maybe it had been a while since she initiated a job search on her own. Maybe the job-search process was overwhelming when combined with a demanding job and family obligations. (Life doesn't stop just because you want to make a career move.) Whatever the reason, Alicia seemed to think that all she had to do was meet me and I would magically pull a job out of some recruiting hat. If that's really what she thought, then she was probably disappointed by my suggestion: She had to do her homework. ●

TO GET A JOB YOU NEED A PLAN

Instead of starting off on a random search, you need to be systematic. In other words, you need a plan, broken down into different phases. Think of it as a marketing strategy in which *you* are the product. You're selling based on your KF4D— who you are and the unique contribution you bring to an employer.

At the same time, you're not just a seller. You're also a buyer. You're buying the right opportunity at an organization whose purpose you're aligned with. This kind of thinking changes things, because it emphasizes the amount of choice you have in the matter. The more work you do on targeting, the better you will be able to market yourself and not waste time on opportunities that aren't a fit—for you or the organization. Your confidence will increase, because you're no longer victimized by what you might perceive as limited opportunities. You take your power back as you focus on what you want and the contribution you can make. ●

> **Your targeting plan is a marketing strategy in which you are the product.**

YOUR TARGETING PLAN

Your plan must include these three main points:

GEOGRAPHY

Where you want to live and work

COMPANIES

Where you would like to work and why—with special attention paid to purpose, culture, and fit

ROLES AND RESPONSIBILITIES

What you can do for your next employer

GEOGRAPHY: WHERE YOU WANT TO LIVE AND WORK

Telling you to know where you want to live and work might seem like obvious advice, but you'd be surprised by how many people don't put enough consideration into location. Over the years, Korn Ferry recruiters have encountered this frustrating problem with hundreds, maybe thousands, of job candidates.

Mary, an executive in Denver, was interviewing for a once-in-a-lifetime dream job in Los Angeles. From the first conversation with the recruiter, Mary gave ample assurances that the move was no problem. She loved California—or at least the *idea* of California: the weather, the ocean, the lifestyle. What could be more perfect?

At the first in-person interview, Mary was asked by the human-resources and hiring managers if relocation was an issue. Once again, her assurance was solid: "No problem."

Through the second and third interviews all systems remained "go" for Mary. The company made an offer, but she didn't respond right away. When the recruiter called to see if there were any issues, Mary came clean. "I didn't tell my partner that the job was in Los Angeles and we'd have to move," she said. "He doesn't want to go."

Unable to come to an agreement with her partner, Mary had to decline the offer. It was a tremendous inconvenience for all involved, especially the company, which had been assured all along that Mary was willing to relocate. When I spoke with Mary a few months ago, she was still in Denver but separated from her partner. She could never get over her resentment toward him for being unwilling to relocate.

This true story is a cautionary tale. Think before you act! The implications are greater than what is happening in the moment. If you turn down an offer at the last minute, that news gets around and could hurt your chances of being hired someplace else. Industries are more tightly knit than you think. Equally important, you don't want to waste your time and energy on opportunities that aren't going to work for you. You need to focus and target the best opportunities.

Commuting is another major issue that people often don't give enough thought to. Before you take a job, you might convince yourself that a ninety-minute or two-hour commute each way is doable. But over time, it can become a serious lifestyle problem. A long daily commute will distort your view of your job and your employer. Resentment will set in, and your performance will suffer—and so, most likely, will your home life. I know of several executives who left rewarding jobs in organizations they admired simply because they couldn't take the commute any longer.

ESTABLISH YOUR GROUND RULES

Know where you want to live and work.
If you want or need to stay in a certain region, state, or city, then don't look at jobs that require you to live and work somewhere else. If you say to a recruiter, "I can go anywhere," make sure that's the truth.

Don't assume that your company will let you work virtually.
While some employers do offer that flexibility, more are requiring employees to spend at least some time in a physical location in order to promote collaboration.

Working in one location and commuting home on the weekends is not a long-term solution.
That might work for a while, and there are plenty of people who have done it, including consultants who might be at a client site Monday through Thursday for a period of several months. But I don't know anybody who can do it indefinitely. Years ago, I knew an oil-industry executive who took a job at a Houston-based trading operation while his family stayed in Connecticut so his young children wouldn't have to change schools. He commuted for a year, then simply couldn't do it any longer and left his job. He told me, "After my last flight, I threw my suitcases away. I literally couldn't stand the sight of them." •

MY GEOGRAPHY WISH LIST

Primary Where do I most want to live and work?

Secondary Which markets would also be acceptable to me?

Questions to Consider

Am I willing to relocate? Why or why not?

Have I considered the cost of living, housing, schools, community, activities, culture?

How long of a commute can I tolerate?

Am I open to a job in a market that's outside my primary and secondary locations?

If so, then what are my criteria for being open to such a move (for example, working for a company whose mission/values I admire and in a position that accelerates my learning)?

YOUR COMPANY WISH LIST

Once you've set your geography target, it's time to move on to the next step of identifying the organizations you'd like to work for. Remember, you're a "buyer," so think about your ideal employer.

MY ORGANIZATION TARGETS

Size of organization: Do I prefer small, medium, or large firms?

Environment/Culture: How would I describe the environment/culture that best suits me (fast-paced, collaborative, casual, corporate, etc.)?

Some very simple questions can give you indications of the type of organization where you'd feel most comfortable. Here are two examples:

WHAT DO YOU WANT TO WEAR TO WORK?

For some people, casual rules. For others, the idea of hoodies or yoga pants is unappealing. How people dress reveals volumes about company culture, and how well you'd fit in. For example, Philip had a doctorate in computer science that would have made him very valuable to a Silicon Valley startup or one of the large, well-established technology firms. But when Philip thought about going to work, he pictured himself in a suit and tie. Not surprisingly, he found the right fit for himself in an investment bank.

WHAT DO YOU LIKE TO READ?

Imagine you're in a reception area with a rack full of magazines. Are you more likely to choose *The Economist* or *The Onion*?

HERE ARE SOME OTHER QUESTIONS TO PONDER

Is working remotely non-negotiable for you?

Do you prefer a sound studio or a library? How would you feel about walking into an office where you could hear a pin drop, or where you could hear music playing and multiple conversations going on at once?

How formal an environment do you prefer? Do you want reserved parking spots, offices with names on the doors, specific scheduled times to meet with people?

Do you like company picnics and holiday parties? Do you like an environment in which people know each other's families?

Do you like the idea of daily communal lunches that come with the expectation you'll spend long hours at your desk?

What does your ideal workplace look like at seven in the morning? Seven at night? How full is the parking lot during the off hours?

Are you open to frequent business travel? How much is too much?

Your answers will give you insights into the kind of environment and the type of company where you'd feel most comfortable. Don't judge yourself or your responses. If you do, you might be tempted to answer in the way you think you should. A lack of authenticity with yourself, however, can lead you to pursuing companies where you won't be a good fit. •

GETTING FEEDBACK ON WHERE YOU BELONG

In addition to asking yourself questions, you can speak with former bosses, colleagues and/or trusted advisors about the kinds of companies where they think you'd thrive. Here are two ways to get the lowdown on the kind of company where you belong:

Contact a former boss, someone who has supervised or managed you in the past, and ask what he or she thinks of your skill set and where you'd be a good fit. Where have people with similar experiences and skills gone, in terms of companies and positions? Does this lay out a career path that makes sense for you? Your former boss's perspective may affirm your own ideas, or it could expand your thinking about possible opportunities.

Seek out a former colleague or someone you know who has joined one of your target companies or a similar firm in the industry. What is it like working there? How would he or she describe the culture? This is different from asking that person to "put in a good word" for you with HR or a hiring manager. That may happen in time, but for now you're looking for the inside scoop on what it's like to work for that company. One of the questions you'll want to ask is, "Who typically gets promoted—do people move upward based on seniority, or is it a meritocracy?" This will give you further insight into the company culture (traditional and hierarchical or flatter and more performance driven) as well as what your career path might be like.

This requires some real homework. You need to look at as many companies as possible (one Korn Ferry career coach recommends investigating fifty companies), so that you can make an informed choice. Depending on what your targeting plan looks like, you could have two lists, which is what Margaret had. After twenty years on Wall Street, she targeted opportunities in two distinct areas. She continued to look at financial services firms, but she was also drawn to philanthropy, which was aligned with her purpose and provided opportunities to apply her investment expertise. As a result, she had two target tracks, each with multiple companies/organizations.

WILL THE COMPANY MOTIVATE YOU?

One final thing to think about at this stage is motivation. It is trendy to say that motivation in the workplace is falling dramatically and consequently companies are losing billions of dollars. While the part about losing billions is true, motivation is a more complex issue. Our research shows that contrary to popular belief, a surprisingly high percentage of people feel internally motivated to go that extra mile. But 40 percent say their company doesn't offer the right incentives to keep them motivated. This gap between the levels of "intrinsic" and "extrinsic" motivation is more than just fodder for cocktail-party talk. It means you're going to be a lot happier if you target companies that provide people with incentive. So dig deep with your research to find out from some of your targets' employees— happy and disgruntled ones—how well the companies recognize and encourage initiative and innovation. ●

40%
SAY THEIR COMPANY DOESN'T OFFER THE RIGHT INCENTIVES TO KEEP THEM MOTIVATED

TARGETING INDUSTRIES AND SECTORS

As you come up with your target companies, the industries and sectors will be an influence. For example, if you are a health-care professional, you will most likely want to work for a health-care company. But for many jobs—especially in the dynamic technology sector—industry is a far more inclusive concept.

When you think of technology companies, the usual names probably come to mind: Amazon, Apple, Google, Facebook, Microsoft, and so forth. Increasingly, though, *every* company is in the technology business. Blue-chip industrial companies, for example, are actively launching digital strategies. Do your homework to discover companies in your geographic targets (or beyond them if you're willing to relocate) that are doing interesting, purpose-driven things. You might be pleasantly surprised at the opportunities that can be found in many corners of today's technologically driven world.

WHERE TO FIND COMPANIES

Conduct a broad Internet search: Searches for "top fifty companies" in a certain city will yield you lists of employers.

Search by geography and sector: If your education (for example, you are a registered nurse), expertise, or area of interest is very specific, then search for companies and organizations that match your specialization (engineering, nursing, teaching) within a specific geographic area.

LinkedIn: Searching LinkedIn for industries or sectors will give you a look at companies and the people who work at them.

Glassdoor: It provides reviews of companies by current and former employees.

Specialized sites: These include Crunchbase for startups and Manta for small businesses.

Alumni sites and groups: Your college alma mater may offer career resources for alumni as well as graduating seniors. These can include networking events and opportunities to hear speakers from various industries and companies.

KNOW WHAT'S MOST IMPORTANT TO YOU

As you target companies, think about what's *most* important to you. For example, if you're passionate about diversity, target companies that have a reputation for being diverse, not only in their workforce, but also within their leadership teams and among board members.

If work/life balance is most important, then consider both the industry and the type of company that would best fit your needs. Investment banking and consulting, for example, are known for long hours, nights and weekends of work. *Know yourself— your desires and your limitations.* The clearer you are about what you need, the better you'll determine the right fit for yourself.

1	2	3
WHAT IS THE REPUTATION OF THE COMPANY?	WHAT DOES THE POSITION REQUIRE OF YOU? (Don't just read the job description. Talk to people who are actually doing the work!)	WORK/LIFE BALANCE?

As you investigate companies and organizations for your list, consider their reputation as employers. Are they a "most admired" company? *Fortune* magazine puts out a list every year, along with its criteria for judging and ranking companies. Several outlets publish rankings of "the best places to work," overall and in a variety of categories (for women, working parents, etc.). Culture is one of the most important criteria when evaluating a company. A company culture can evolve over time, but probably not fast enough if you find yourself in a situation that doesn't fit you.

> **People are hired for what they know— but fired for who they are! Make sure who you are fits the company culture.**

At Korn Ferry, we've hired a few executives who were eager to work for the firm but not ready to commit to the nights and weekends that often come with this job. One executive, after he was hired, refused to take calls on Saturday, wanted a parking spot with his name on it, and went to the gym every day at 2:30. Needless to say, this did not work out.

You can find out a lot about company culture through online research. The company's own website is a good place to start. There you can read the company's mission and vision statements and research its philanthropic activities.

Your Job-Search Checklist

1. Research the industries that interest you, where you have experience, and/or where your competencies are in demand.

2. Identify companies in those industries.

3. Research the culture at the companies by visiting each one's site and by reading about them in news stories and blogs and on message boards.

4. Search your network for people who work at these companies or know others who do.

How is the company regarded in its industry? Investigate the company's Facebook and LinkedIn pages and check out blogs posted by the company. Follow your targeted companies on Twitter. Social media will also allow you to see comments by current and former employees. And if you comment on a blog post written by a current employee, it could be the start of a connection that gets you an introduction.

If the company is publicly traded, it will be followed by Wall Street analysts, whose research reports will be available on financial websites such as Yahoo Finance. You can listen in on earnings calls or recordings of the calls. What do the customer reviews say about the company's products and services?

As you comb the company's site, look at the board and the leadership team. Where did senior executives work previously? Where did they go to school? Your detective work continues. Look at their LinkedIn profiles and see if there are any useful connections. *Do they know someone who knows someone, who knows someone, who might know me?* (Make note of these connections, which you'll put to good use in "networking.") Check out these leaders on social media and on blogs.

What job openings are listed on the company site? What kind of talent are they looking for? All these insights will help you compile and refine your company list. ●

THE JOB-SEARCH SPIRAL: ROLES AND RESPONSIBILITIES

As you come to the next phase—targeting specific roles and responsibilities—your job search can be narrowly or broadly defined, depending on your expertise and experience level. Generally speaking, the more time you've spent in one industry or one type of functional role, the more unlikely it is that you're going to make a drastic career move. But at the entry level and mid level, you do have more latitude in the roles you pursue and the industries and sectors you target.

It's like a spiral, with your current job in the center. If your job search is limited to opportunities based on your direct experience—doing the same job for a similar company—you will not move too far out on the spiral. You may go to a larger competitor or manage a larger team or bigger projects. Even when the move is closely related to your current job, know what you're seeking. How much responsibility are you ready to take on? Do you want to be a team member or a team leader? Are you looking to manage people? Do you want to have responsibility for P&L (profit and loss), or are you an individual contributor?

Or you may look at a neighboring sector. You're in pharmaceuticals, but you're interested in medical devices; or you're in banking and you're interested in brokerage. These sectors are closely related, so you're only one turn out on the spiral. With well-defined competencies and skills and experiences that demonstrate what you can contribute, you probably won't find it difficult to be taken seriously by a hiring manager.

The same applies to changing roles within the same sector. You're a marketing manager for a B2B technology company, but you'd like to pursue a B2B sales role. The closer you are to the center of the spiral, the more logical the career move will seem.

Some people, however, pursue dramatic changes that put them farther out on the spiral. Generally speaking, the more you move away from your center, the harder it is to translate your skill set and industry knowledge. That said, there are specific roles and areas of expertise that are in high demand across industries. These include data analytics, digital supply-chain management, and cybersecurity. To obtain the expertise they need, some companies will actively recruit from other industries.

But if you are looking to change industries because you're interested in something completely different, it will be more difficult. For one thing, you'll be facing competition from people who have a background that more closely matches what the company is looking for. It's not impossible, but it will take hard work on your part to make such a change. Here's how you can get started:

A "Reality" Check-In

If you've done well in your current company, receiving several promotions, you may need a reality check about how you should market yourself outside the firm. Since your career path, until now, has comprised only internal moves, you probably haven't had to figure out where you fit and what jobs are right for you. If that's the case, here's an exercise suggested by one of our recruiters: Imagine you're going to leave your job in two months and set up a consulting business. What services would you provide, or what products would you sell? Who would be your target customers? What companies in what industries would be your biggest clients?

Network: Find out all you can about your "new" industry from people in that field. Don't start out by asking about jobs that might be suitable for you. Instead, focus on what that person does. Ask about his or her role and responsibilities. What's a typical day like? Who are the customers? What's the culture like?

Translate your experiences: Once you understand the kind of expertise valued within your new industry, think about how you can contribute. How does what you've done translate into expertise this industry needs?

Know what your perspective brings: How does coming from another industry make you an attractive candidate? Has your industry gone through similar challenges (rapid expansion, consolidation, digital transformation, etc.) that this new industry is now facing?

No matter how close to the center you remain or far out you go on the job-search spiral, it's all about what you bring to your next employer. Based on your most recent jobs and the accomplishments you've achieved, what are you known for—what makes you unique? •

THE PIVOT POINT

Remember Jed, the former SVP who discovered his megaphone for getting noticed was far too tiny? What would he say about all this? In truth, most people who dive into this often-ignored but critical step of targeting their next opportunity start off far more confident than Jed was and a lot less depressed. Targeting is much more than job-market research. It is the pivot in your job-search process from understanding who you are and the value you bring (your KF4D) to where that value is likely to be recognized and appreciated. You won't be shooting darts blindfolded, going after any job out of desperation and frustrating yourself in the process. You'll pursue opportunities that make sense to you (and to the prospective hiring manager)—which can improve your chances of landing a job that will continue and even accelerate your career trajectory. ●

NETWORKING IS A CONTACT SPORT

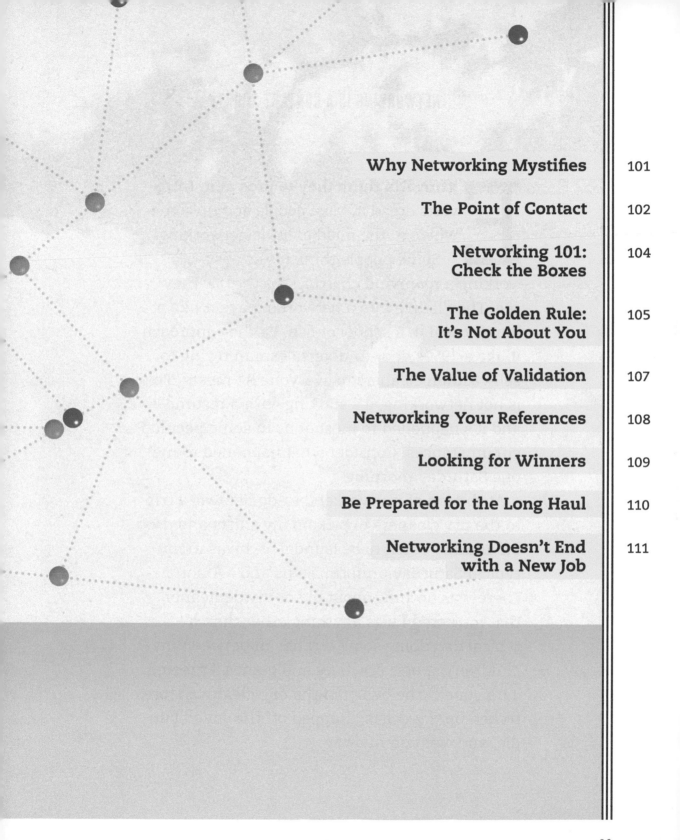

NETWORKING IS A CONTACT SPORT

Extroverts think they're pros at it. Introverts dread it. Most people end up somewhere in the middle. "It" is networking.

Some people think it's as easy as working a room and chatting up *everyone* they see. They'll dive into a networking event like a hungry seal in a school of fish. Or they approach it like a 1950s door-to-door salesman trying to sell vacuum cleaners to everyone he meets. This is not networking; it's stalking with a resume—and it's happened to most of us in some peculiar circumstances. Consider what happened to me one Saturday morning.

At the top of my weekend to-do list was a trip to the dry cleaners to pick up my shirts and drop off another batch to be laundered. I was in my typical Saturday uniform: jeans and a T-shirt. There was nothing about me or my demeanor that indicated I was anything other than a typical dad doing some errands in between my children's sports practices and games. I greeted "Mrs. Jones," the owner of the dry-cleaning store, picked up my shirts, dropped off the soiled bundle, and went on my way.

The Unspoken Truth

✖

Networking is a big mystery to most people. And even many of those who *think* they do it well probably don't— because they don't realize it's always about the other person.

WHY NETWORKING MYSTIFIES

But later that day, as I hung up the clean shirts in my closet, I made a startling discovery. Slipped between two of my shirts was a resume for "John Jones," a recent college graduate and, it appeared, Mrs. Jones's son.

Mrs. Jones and I never had a conversation. She never told me she had a son or that he was in college. She never asked if I would take a few minutes to give her son some career advice. And quite frankly, I don't know how she knew I was with Korn Ferry. Maybe she had wondered why I wore so many dress shirts and googled my name.

But honestly, surreptitiously placing a resume in my shirts was nothing short of bizarre. It was not networking. (By the way, I did eventually meet and have coffee with the son. He's a good kid with a promising future.) •

Knowing how to network effectively is a big mystery to most people, I've decided, because they dread it so much. They feel awkward asking for help, and the idea of reaching out to someone has all the appeal of cold-calling to sell those handy slice-and-dice-it knives you see on late-night infomercials. That's not networking, folks!

This raises an even bigger point: Net-working poorly is worse than not networking at all. A second case in point: I was in the hospital for an outpatient procedure—nothing major, but the kind of thing that requires anesthesia and a little recovery time afterward. As I lay there in my attractive light-blue hospital gown with an IV in my arm, an anesthesiologist came in to see me.

I was expecting more questions about how I felt and the last time I ate or drank anything. Instead, the anesthesiologist smiled, checked my chart, and asked me what I did for a living. When I told him, he said, "Oh, I could never do that—way too much pressure!"

The next thing I knew, the procedure was over, and I was being taken on a gurney to the recovery room. Even in my groggy state, it registered that the anesthesiologist was wheeling me. This seemed unusual, and I wondered if something was wrong. "Everything okay?" I murmured.

Seeing I was awake, the anesthesiologist gave me a big, reassuring smile. Then he reached into his white coat and pulled out a two-page document. Blurry-eyed, I couldn't believe what I was seeing. It was his resume. "When you mentioned Korn Ferry," he said, "I figured it couldn't hurt."

Really? I may have been a "captive audience," but I wasn't exactly in a frame of mind to network.

Networking foibles show just how bad many people are at this. Consider the experience of one of our recruiters who, while at the gym, was suddenly greeted in the sauna by someone he didn't know. "I hear you're a recruiter," said the man, an IT professional who had been out of work for eight months. "I'd like to tell you more about myself."

"Do you see any place I might be carrying a pen?" the recruiter asked.

The man took the hint and left with his steam-wilted resume.

Such ambush attempts are really a turnoff! But you can't go to the other extreme either and avoid networking altogether. Networking is vitally important to getting your next job. But you must do it right and in a way that's adapted to the time-pressed, tech-savvy world we live in.

As an ongoing exercise, networking involves far more than just thinking about asking everyone you know if they know of any job openings. This kind of networking is usually an exercise in futility. You'll waste your time and everyone else's. And you can't keep knocking on the same doors, asking people to help you. At some point you'll wear out even your friends. ●

THE POINT OF CONTACT

That's why networking shouldn't begin when you're looking for a job. If you haven't thought about the care and nurturing of your network until now, you're behind the curve. Connecting with people for the sole purpose of asking their help will put off many of them—especially if they don't know you well. It's just human nature.

I hadn't seen or heard from "Joe" in more than a dozen years. While we worked in the same industry, our paths seldom crossed, other than in the most tangential way at industry events. And we were not friends outside of work. What I did know about Joe was from the financial news: Several years ago, he pleaded guilty to insider trading and spent a few months in jail.

Never during that time did he reach out to me. Never in that time did anyone we knew in common reach out to me. He was a distant memory and a familiar name in a newspaper article about an unfortunate incident.

So imagine my surprise when more than a decade after our last contact, Joe emails me, requesting we "get together for lunch." He

> **Connecting with people for the sole purpose of asking for their help will put off many of them—especially if they don't know you well.**

needed a job and was hoping I could give him some advice and introduce him to some of our recruiters. Really?

My reaction had nothing to do with the fact that Joe spent time in prison for insider trading. From what I read, he took full responsibility for what had happened. Rather, it was because his first contact with me—after so many years and given the fact that we weren't more than nodding acquaintances—was a request to "pick my brain" about getting a job.

You may think I'm being harsh, but this is the reaction you're going to get from other people if you approach them "out of the blue." You may find someone who, for whatever reason, will help. But, quite frankly, that will be the exception and not the norm. •

MORE THAN JUST A NAME

KORN FERRY'S global network of consultants are a pretty popular bunch. Their networks are broad and deep, especially in the industries or functional areas in which they specialize. It's their job to know everyone! As one of our recruiters told me recently, "I make a strong effort to get to know all the contacts in my network." She's met hundreds of people through career placements, industry events, and/or LinkedIn, and she can tell you something about each of them—how she met them, the projects they worked on, and topics they're interested in. These contacts are more than just names. They're real people!

Think about this as you build your network. LinkedIn can be a great tool, but you shouldn't reach out to "connect" unless you really know someone. Otherwise you're just a name, and your request to connect likely will be ignored.

NETWORKING 101: CHECK THE BOXES

Much has been written on the rudiments of networking. But here are the basics. A word of advice (or consider it a warning): To get a job, you'll need to go way beyond checking these boxes.

[ ] **NETWORKING REQUIRES AN OBJECTIVE**
Have a goal in mind so that your discussions with people have a purpose. When people in your network understand your goals, they'll gain clarity about where and how they can help you. If your objective is to get a new job, make sure your goals are focused on specific organizations and positions.

[ ] **MAKE A LIST**
Write down the names of everyone in your network—family members, friends, current and former colleagues, business contacts, members of professional organizations, people you know socially or through groups you belong to. As you go through the list, think about the people you see regularly.

[ ] **MATCH CONTACTS AND COMPANIES**
As you categorize your contacts, also think about the companies that are at the top of your "wish list" of next employers. Who in your network can connect you to someone in the company?

[ ] **BE RESPECTFUL OF OTHER PEOPLE'S TIME**
When you reach out to people in your network—whether to "pick their brains" about a company or to request an introduction to someone—they are doing you a favor. Even if that contact is a good friend, you can wear out that person by constantly nagging for help. Chances are people will do what they can, but it's up to you to do the heavy lifting.

THE GOLDEN RULE: IT'S NOT ABOUT YOU

Networking is about building rela-tionships—and relationships aren't one-way streets. That's why the golden rule about networking is: *It's not about you!* Ideally, networking is grounded in what you can do for others. You can't be the person calling out of nowhere who asks for help from someone you haven't spoken to in five years! It happens all too often, and it's a blatant misuse of your network. You can't take out what you haven't put in.

Right now, make a list of the possible things you can do for people in your net-work. Even small things, if done sincerely and if they are genuinely meaningful to the other person (and those are two significant ifs), can jump-start your networking. You're building goodwill with others for the day when you need help.

This is real networking—and it's all about what you can give to others. And you can call it karma, paying it forward, or a reward for a job well done—I call it the fruits of networking—but when you need their help, the people you've helped in the past will be more than happy to step up.

Of course, it's not always that simple. Networking can be a psychological bal-ancing act. A vice president at Korn Ferry once told me how he used to make a habit of contacting colleagues who had just lost their jobs. To be sure, the gesture was nice, but he confessed that—after a couple of hand-holding lunches—he knew he could reach out to them when they found a new job. Indeed, this "magnanimous" move got him in the door of two Fortune 500 firms. "Should I feel guilty?" he asked out loud.

Maybe, but there are other examples of "sincere" gestures prompted by ulterior motives, subconsciously or not. Bosses and managers dread laying off people, but the good ones will make an effort to find those workers other jobs. It might occur to some bosses that years later, that laid-off person may end up running a company. It's a stark reality that we all must recognize: Someone shown the door could be the person who can let you in someday. •

Networking is about building relationships—and relationships aren't one-way streets.

10 THINGS YOU CAN DO FOR YOUR NETWORK
(WHICH YOU SHOULD HAVE BEEN DOING ALREADY)

1

WHO CAN YOU HELP? Do you know someone else who is looking for a job? If so, reach out and offer to help, from brainstorming ideas to introducing him or her to someone you know.

2

WHO IN YOUR NETWORK HAS SIMILAR INTERESTS TO EACH OTHER'S—PROFESSIONALLY OR PERSONALLY—AND WOULD BENEFIT FROM MEETING? If you're all local, arrange to have coffee together. Or suggest that you connect them by email (with each party's permission).

3

WHOSE CHILD CAN YOU OFFER TO HELP? Maybe you've heard that the son or daughter of someone you know is thinking of applying to your alma mater, or is looking to enter a field similar to yours.

4

WHO HAS WRITTEN A BLOG THAT YOU CAN SHARE WITHIN YOUR SOCIAL MEDIA NETWORK? Or can you leave a meaningful reply to the post? (This one is especially helpful if you are networking "up" the line with someone a few levels above you.)

5

IF YOU BLOG, WHO CAN YOU INTERVIEW TO GAIN THEIR PERSPECTIVE ON A TOPIC? If your blog is well followed, this can help establish your contacts as subject-matter experts.

6

WHAT SKILL DO YOU HAVE TO OFFER SOMEONE? Are you good at social media? Can you help set up a simple website? Can you be a sounding board for someone who is launching a business or a new project?

7

WHO SHOULD YOU CONGRATULATE? Think of someone with a particular accomplishment or life event— a new job, an engagement or marriage, a new house.

8

CAN YOU RECOMMEND A NEW RESTAURANT, ART GALLERY, OR EVEN A GOOD BOOK TO SOMEONE IN YOUR NETWORK? Don't make your recommendation seem random. Let the person know why you thought of him or her.

9

WHO CAN YOU INVITE TO A PROFESSIONAL OR CULTURAL EVENT? This is a great way to reconnect with former colleagues or other people you haven't seen in a while.

10

DO YOU KNOW SOMEONE WHO IS INVOLVED IN A CHARITY OR COMMUNITY EVENT AND NEEDS A VOLUNTEER? Giving of yourself, even for a few hours, is an excellent way to nurture your network and meet new people in a different context.

THE VALUE OF VALIDATION

A **Harvard graduate. A West Point** graduate. A Navy SEAL. A professional athlete. If any of these distinctions describe you, congratulations. In the words of Don Corleone, you've been "made."

But these instant validations distinguish a very small minority. Consider that Harvard University lists 371,000 living alumni. Now compare that number with the 160 million people in the U.S. workforce. That's less than 0.25 percent.

For most of us, validation must come from another source. As you build and nurture your network, you are also building relationships with people who will validate you. Often these contacts are former bosses and current and former colleagues. These are people who know you from working and interacting with you. When they attest to your skills, your accomplishments, and your contribution as a team member or team leader, their words carry weight.

In addition, as you're networking, you're building your reputation—your expertise, your presence (your poise and grooming, how you interact with others), and your personality. All these factors come together when you need someone to vouch for you in a way that opens the door to your next job. Ideally, here's how this works:

There's an opening for a job you really want at the company that's the ideal fit

A Job Where There Isn't an Opening

One of the best possible outcomes is landing a job that did not exist before. Companies are always in the market for talent at every level. Even if there are no openings or a company has a hiring freeze, the right talent can usually find a home.

This is where all your hard work—targeting the right opportunities and networking with others—opens doors. The best way for this to happen is with a "warm introduction" to people inside the company. Through formal meetings or informal get-togethers, you'll give people a sense of your "likability," along with your direct experience, competencies, and skills.

This is where everything comes together: who you are, what you bring, your motivation, and where you want to go. There are so many possibilities to explore, but only if you are willing to invest the time and effort to make things happen for yourself.

for you. Your traits and competencies make you a great candidate for the position. Your experiences paint a picture of career progression that makes this job the logical next step. Instead of just throwing your resume into the stream, you search your network of contacts for someone to vouch for you.

It may be someone you know directly, or you may have to network your way to get to "someone who knows someone." If your path is indirect, you're probably going to have a conversation with that contact. No one is going to vouch for you unless he or she knows you. But when you find someone who is willing to "put in a good word for you" with the HR department or the hiring manager, you'll be so much further ahead than the other candidates.

You'll still have to fill out the online forms and submit your resume so that you're in the system. But that's not what's going to get you in the door for an interview. You'll get the interview because your contact is willing to put his or her reputation on the line to vouch for you. •

NETWORKING YOUR REFERENCES

As everyone who's ever applied for a job knows, providing references is part of the process. And as we'll discuss in later chapters, companies often do deep due diligences (especially for senior positions) when it comes to checking references—listed and unlisted. Long before you're asked to provide references by a prospective employer, you should know who they are. (You might be shocked to learn how few people have them lined up ahead of time.) Don't choose references just because they're likely to say "good things" about you. Choose people who can comment substantively about you, how you work, and how you interact with and lead others.

Choose people who can comment substantively about you.

To identify these people, you need to network with them first through meaningful contact. (Once again, this will be easier if you've been actively networking all along.) For example, let's assume you've kept in touch with a former boss or supervisor. Let him or her know that you're engaging in some career exploration. Given your experience and skill set, what does your former boss think is a logical next step for you?

This type of networking is a valuable self-assessment, and it helps you identify references who can speak meaningfully about your strengths and weaknesses. •

Conducting Your Own 360-Degree

Companies frequently use 360-degree assessments to gather feedback from all levels: bosses, peers, and direct reports. In your networking, you can mimic the 360-degree approach to gain insights.

1. Ask a former boss or supervisor for feedback about your strengths or weaknesses. "If I were still working for you, where would I be assigned now?"

2. Contact a former colleague for feedback about how you interact with others. "If you were putting together a team, what role or position would you assign to me?"

3. A former direct report can give you insights about how you were perceived by the team. "Did people feel championed by me? If so, how?"

LOOKING FOR WINNERS

Not only is validation good for you, it's also valuable from the *company's perspective*. Just as you want someone in your target company to vouch for you, that employer is glad to get an insider's recommendation about you. When someone speaks for you, the hiring manager has greater confidence in your abilities and your fit with the culture.

As we mentioned before, it costs so much to recruit and hire people—as much as $1 million to replace a single senior executive—and the cost of a bad hire is even greater. To reduce hiring risk, companies want to know as much as they can about candidates. For example, do you have a bona fide track record of accomplishments—those quantifiable contributions you've made to the organizations for which you've worked. Companies want to have confidence that you are who you say you are and that your trajectory is real. (That's why reference checks must be more than a perfunctory exercise for companies, as we'll discuss in later chapters.) They are looking for evidence that you have, indeed, been on an upward career path—managing more people, generating more business, taking on more responsibilities. These are the signs of someone who is an outlier of achievement, with a winning track record that's verifiable. And just as important, companies are looking for culture fit. •

BE PREPARED FOR THE LONG HAUL

Iread a column in a well-known business publication that presented a twelve-week plan for getting a new job. (Those twelve weeks included three weeks to score interview number one. "High five!") My only promise is that job hunts are almost always longer and more painful than you expect. You'll send more emails, make more phone calls, leave more messages, and wait for longer periods than you can imagine. The best advice from our recruiters is to prepare yourself physically and mentally for that wait.

But what does that really mean? Physical preparation means burning off steam, which should mean exercising. I must warn you, though, that even some very active people end up doing less when they are out of work, because job hunting saps their energy and their morale. It's the ones who continue to push through who have an edge, because exercise clears their head, relieves frustration, and generates endorphins that keep them positive. If you can't manage to work out, there's also the option

Don't Check Out Early

One of the realities of today's job market is the frequency of job-hopping. People change jobs an average of four times by the time they are thirty-two years old. This means a lot of *leaving* companies. It also means a lot of chances to fall into one of the biggest pitfalls of career building: leaving badly.

We're all familiar with the scenario: Your work colleague starts coming in later and later, and leaving assignments for others to deal with. Meanwhile, he has let down the boss, too, by missing deadlines. It turns out he accepted a job weeks ago and has wrongly assumed that what happens in the waning days of his current job won't matter. But people's reputations follow them, and bad departures may ruin years of developing future references. It's remarkable, in fact, how many people think their colleagues or supervisor will someday forget their behavior, or that they will never need references from them. Trust me, the workplace world is always smaller than you think.

of breathing exercises or meditation—or taking a walk or going fishing. Anything will help.

The mental preparation is a little trickier. According to one survey, more than a fifth of the unemployed suffer from depression, and 27 percent report sadness. These are stark numbers that show having the willpower to stay positive is critical. Don't invite the negative thoughts to come over and play in your head. The truth is, people want to help winners. The minute you come across as defeated, people will be less enthusiastic about recommending you because they will doubt your confidence. A recommendation that doesn't work out will reflect badly on them. (We've all had that happen.) Once burned, people will avoid risking that mistake again.

There will be times when you'll need someone to listen to you vent. Take your frustrations elsewhere, away from anyone who could recommend you for a job. And while we're at it, it's probably not advisable to use your spouse or partner for venting, either. Job transitions can be stressful on relationships. Adding to that stress by moaning that you'll never get another job probably isn't going to help at home.

Instead, find someone else to support you—a listening ear when you need some cheering up or a sounding board when you're frustrated. This may mean a career coach, who can advise you through the process. You can also look for a job-search buddy (but not from your company), another person who's going through the same thing. You can share stories and experiences that keep you both motivated. •

NETWORKING DOESN'T END WITH A NEW JOB

My last word on networking is to remember this is an ongoing process. It doesn't end when you get a new job. You must keep giving to your network—helping others, engaging with them via social media, and doing the other "ten things" we highlighted. Because here's the secret that no one talks about: As soon as you land your job, you need to think about the next one. That's the progression that will keep your career trajectory on track. •

YOUR RESUME: THE STORY YOU TELL

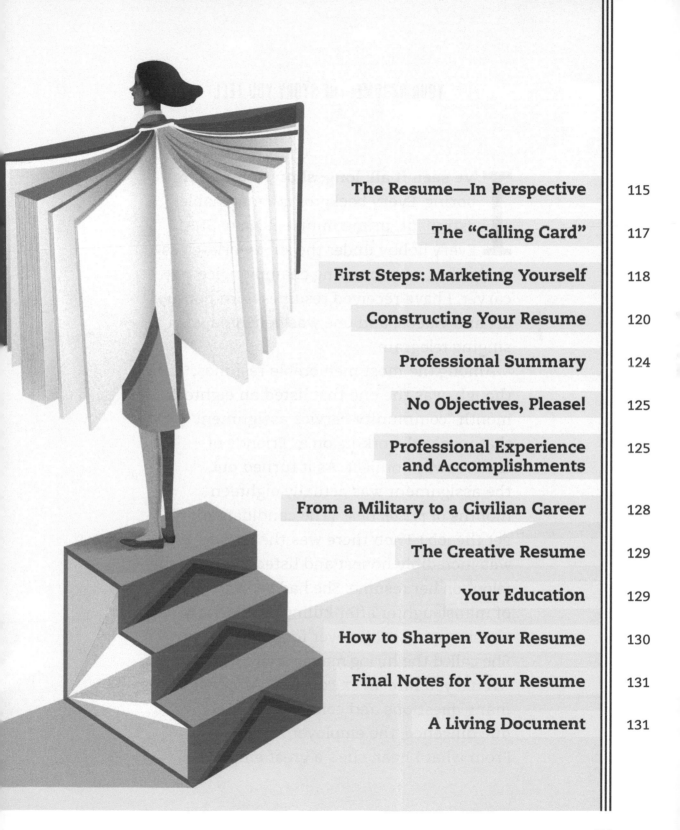

YOUR RESUME: THE STORY YOU TELL

I've seen it all: long, short, interesting, boring. Every background imaginable: astronaut, prime minister, Navy SEAL. Every hobby under the sun: world-class sushi chef, axe-throwing champion, ice carver. I have received resumes with pop-up art and videos, and one was delivered with a singing telegram.

Among the most memorable resumes, though, was the one that listed an eighteen-month "community-service assignment" that involved working on a "Friends of the Freeway" project. As it turned out, the assignment was actually eighteen months of *prison time*. (The candidate didn't get the job.) Then there was the person who was incredibly honest and listed "convicted felon" on her resume. She had been convicted of manslaughter after killing her horribly abusive spouse. I'll never forget the story: She called the hiring manager and asked, "Would you hire an ex-convict?" After asking many questions and conducting extensive due diligence, the employer hired her. From what I hear, she's a great employee.

THE RESUME— IN PERSPECTIVE

Early in my career, I was introduced by someone in my network to a hiring manager at a company I wanted to work for. When the manager invited me to send a copy of my resume (in those days, by U.S. mail), I spent countless hours writing and polishing it. I wanted my resume to be perfect. When it came time for the in-person interview, the hiring manager opened our conversation with the usual icebreaker: "So, tell me about yourself." Immediately, I began reciting the positions I'd held thus far and my responsibilities in each job. The manager interrupted me. "I know what's on your resume," he said. "Tell me about *you*. Tell me a story so I can really know who you are."

This experience was literally career changing— I got the job—and all because I grasped two important things. First, as you know by now from our major premise, your resume alone is not the gateway to a new job. Networking to obtain a

The Unspoken Truth

✖

Your resume will be scanned for only *seconds* at first, and then reviewed for two to five minutes before you come in for an interview. You must make those quick glances count.

"warm introduction" to a company remains the most important job-search activity. Second, what matters most is being able to tell a great story that conveys who you are. Your resume is the introduction to that story.

The resume has lost a lot of its weight over the years to the LinkedIn profile and a positive, professional social-media presence (as we'll discuss in the next chapter). This makes your resume "old-school." Recruiters and hiring managers spend only *seconds* on the initial screening of a resume. Once you make the cut, your resume will get a little longer look, but it's still usually less than five minutes.

Important as an online presence is, you still need a resume, which you will submit when you apply for jobs or contact recruiters. (Recruiters will also check you out online. It's one of the first things they do.)

Ask five people about how to write a great resume and you'll get fifteen different responses. There are countless books and guides out there that focus on how to write a resume. (An Amazon search turned up

Your resume is not a stand-alone document, but part of your brand, which you must define and showcase— mostly online.

twenty *pages* of books on resumes, cover letters, and similar resources.) Given our "lose the resume, land the job" premise, we're not going to engage in a discussion of the merits of Times New Roman versus Calibri typeface.

And for the record, the most difficult, frustrating, and time-consuming part of this entire book was putting together the sample resumes. These resumes took weeks of effort by several people. The irony wasn't lost on us that all this work was for a book called *Lose the Resume*. There were times we wanted to take that advice literally and lose these resume samples! This exercise more than proved the point that writing and revising a resume can make you want to tear your hair out. No wonder people lose focus, slap something together (typos and all), and send it out. We feel your pain—but there is a better way.

The purpose here is to talk about your resume—what it's supposed to do for you and how you can use it to help tell your story. ●

> The most difficult, frustrating, and time-consuming part of writing this entire book was putting together the resume samples—proving the point that writing a resume can make you want to tear your hair out.

Zero-based thinking

☐ Freedom to do what I want, when
✔
✗   I want (including required family things)

☐ Being present and around for my family-
✔   raising the kids & being a great
✗   husband

☐ Having enough $ to pay for what
O? we like to do - now & in the future
✔
    -schools   -vacations
    - club
    -quality of life ☐ having nest egg to
                     support great worry-free
                            retirement

☐ interesting, engaging profession with
✔   intellectual meat on the bone
✔

☐ working with interesting cool people -
✔   without drama & bureaucracy
✗

☐ self-actualization - the freedom,
✔ space, culture and environment
✔- required to enable the development
of original work

☐ being a part of a community that
✔
✔- is uplifting, supportive, &
full of opportunity

☐ supportive of excellent health →
✔   great sleep, great diet, lots of
✔- exercise, no/little, only healthy
stress

"PRODUCTIVE AND FUN!"

☐ DONE AND DONE ☐ TAKING NAMES ☐ KICKING ASS ☐ WEAKSAUCE

LEVEL OF PRODUCTIVITY
(FILL IN HIGHEST LEVEL REACHED)

DO THESE THINGS!	CONTACT THESE PEOPLE!	BUY THIS STUFF!
☐ ALL DONE!	☐ ALL CONTACTED!	☐ ALL BOUGHT!

Handwritten notes:

DO THESE THINGS!
- Network Science
- $12 → 2020
- ups/downs —
- some big deals —
- An italian pension
- as space stack in
- the rails
- Covid backchannel comfort strong

- Can I be successful?
- What have you seen?
- What would you do?
- you in the city culture
- are you serious dawn?
- time for a spiritual tho?

CONTACT THESE PEOPLE!
- Fund in funds
- fund
- h3 shapers/lower end out PE
- v. package
- complex
- Tinium
- meta
- Ste clu

BUY THIS STUFF!
- SWME
- KNSA
- RCCA
- XOMA

PRODUCTIVE AF!

Not every manager or recruiter reads a resume the same way. Some will zero in on keywords, including those flagged by scanning software. Others will look for specific experiences or accomplishments. I read a resume in what may be an atypical way: I look for sequentially bigger titles and more responsibilities. I also focus on company names, seeing the progression of responsibilities from one firm to the next. This often involves just a quick scan, but I know what I'm looking for.

THE "CALLING CARD"

Don't misinterpret the de-emphasis of the resume as permission for you to slap together a document, believing that no one will look at it or pay much attention to it. Even one typo or grammatical error could knock you out of the running.

To get through the HR screening process, you need a solid resume that summarizes your experiences, shows that you match the qualifications of the job you're applying for, and gives a good indication of the quantifiable results you have achieved. That's a lot for the reader to absorb at a glance, so you have to be concise yet thorough—a crucial balance to achieve.

Your resume will also serve as a conversation guide for the in-person interviews. In a Korn Ferry survey of executives, nearly two-thirds (65 percent) said that once resumes have been screened and potential candidates identified, they review the resumes from all those candidates and decide which ones they'd like to meet. This process highlights the sole purpose of your resume: to help you get an interview and to showcase the stories you will want to tell during an in-person meeting. ●

FIRST STEPS: MARKETING YOURSELF

Think of your resume as a marketing document for yourself. By what you present, you're telling recruiters and hiring managers what they're going to get if you're hired for their organization or work on their teams. You're not justifying why you have outgrown your current position and now need to change jobs. Rather, you want to generate enthusiasm about the contribution you can make to their company.

Despite the vast amount of information available on how to write a resume, shockingly few people do it well. Even executives with impressive careers sometimes have resumes that barely distinguish them. The CEO of a large company (one you've heard of) contacted me to ask a favor: Would I look at his resume and critique it? When I received the document, I couldn't believe what I was reading. It was just one *job description* after another.

What this CEO obviously didn't realize is that a resume is more than just a list of every job and its required tasks. Missing from this document were any descriptions of his leadership qualities and the accomplishments that would put into perspective his twenty-plus-year career as a leader. Nowhere on those pages was there anything that brought him to life or gave an indication that he understood his "KF4Ds"—traits, drivers,

> ## ENDS VS. MEANS
>
> ———
>
> **The more senior the person, the briefer each job description, with a greater focus on *the ends achieved*.**
>
> **The more junior the person, the greater the focus on the *means to the ends*.**

competencies, and experiences. All he showed was what he had done, job to job.

A resume needs to "ACT" on your behalf: first, with an *authentic* representation of your accomplishments; next, by using language that makes a *connection* around what motivates you and the sense of purpose you will bring to the organization; and third, by giving people a *taste* of what it will be like to work with you, an impression you will confirm and amplify in person.

That's why we've waited until now, the middle of the book, to discuss resumes. Only after you've done all the hard work of getting to know yourself and your KF4Ds can you write a resume that conveys a compelling story. At this point, you really understand the culture where you would fit best, and you know the kind of boss you want to work for. You appreciate what you've learned thus far and what you need to learn to continue your career trajectory. You have—we hope—a complete understanding of yourself, enabling you to present a resume with a genuine story. •

Five Resume Truths

Clearly, it doesn't take a genius to think of some simple resume truths, but it is worth remembering them:

1
DON'T LIE

2
DON'T INFLATE

3
MIND THE TIME GAPS

4
MAKE IT ATTRACTIVE TO THE EYE

Include white space. Balance bold fonts for names, titles, and names of companies with regular fonts for descriptions. Use bullet points for accomplishments, and include action verbs.

5
SHOWCASE YOUR "BRAND"

Don't think of your resume as a stand-alone document. It's a summary, an outline. Far more important is what you are known for—your brand—which must be continually defined and articulated as the story you tell.

CONSTRUCTING YOUR RESUME

As we were putting together a resume template for this chapter (and for the Appendix, which contains samples for entry-level, professional-level, and C-suite talent), we turned to our experts at Korn Ferry. But even our experts—who see, critique, and give advice on more resumes from people at every professional level than anybody else on the planet—did not have a one-size-fits-all template for a best-in-class resume. This proves the point made earlier about asking five people and getting fifteen opinions. It also raises a larger and more important point: There is no magic formula for a resume that will automatically lead to a job offer.

Keep in mind what your resume is meant to do (and what it cannot do): It serves as a concise summary that showcases your competencies, experience, and accomplishments.

FIVE *LOSE THE RESUME* RESUME RULES

1. No resume format, typography, layout, or keywords will automatically make your next interviewer say, "Wow, we have to hire this person." It's a calling card, folks. Consider the fact that some companies are even resorting to algorithms, instead of resumes, to determine who is the best fit for a position. One global company's foray into this area combines an online application, a series of skill-assessment activities thinly disguised as games, and video-recorded responses to questions. Only after candidates make the initial, tech-driven cut do humans get involved. In this brave new world, your resume will count for less and less. But for now, you must have one.

2. A B+ resume (in terms of format and attractiveness) from someone with A+ experience (involvement with, for example, top-notch consulting firms or Fortune 100 companies) will win over the inverse: a beautifully written A+ resume from someone with only B+ experience. Content and relevancy matter most!

3. Do not distract the HR department or the hiring manager with a creative resume format. In 95 percent of careers, gimmicks will not get you where you want to go. The only exception is if you are pursuing an artistic occupation. If you want to be, say, an art director, stage manager, or graphic designer, you can let your free spirit reign. But even then, content matters.

4. Don't ask your partner/spouse, parent, best friend, or anyone else who loves you to critique your resume. (KF Advance offers resume review and coaching.) The people closest to you—the ones who say, "We believe in you!"—are unlikely to tell you the blunt truth that your resume is gibberish or lacks authenticity. Hire a coach or ask a mentor (such as a former boss in your network) or someone at the alumni/career services office at your alma mater. A resume critique needs to be from someone with a sharp eye and a willingness to give you tough love—not a pep talk.

5. Never, ever describe yourself as "innovative," "energetic," "a team player," "a self-starter," or a "good communicator." These words and terms are so overused they have become meaningless.

With this understanding, let's walk through a sample resume (see page 122). We chose someone at the professional level, *where technical skills still matter.* A resume for someone at the director or manager level (or the equivalent) is likely to be longer and more detailed in terms of technical skills than for someone at the C level, where what matters most is title, company, and accomplishments. And, of course, a professional-level resume contains more than that of an entry-level resume.

Our hypothetical example (the person, the experiences, and the companies listed are not real) is for Jonathan Sample, a financial professional who is currently a controller at a midsize health-care company. (Resumes for Susan Sample, a CEO, and for Grace Sample, who has been in the workforce only a few years, and others can be found in the Appendix.)

First, on the following page, is the entire resume for Jonathan Sample. (Numbers and percentages represented by "X" are to show style and format.)

> **Your resume should concisely and compellingly illustrate one major message point: This is how I made things better for my employer while I was there.**

Jonathan Sample

4444 Century Park South, Apt 444
Dallas, TX 75001
Cell: (214) 000-0000
jsample@sample.com

PROFESSIONAL SUMMARY

Financial executive with extensive experience building and leading teams.
Areas of expertise include:

- Strategic planning
- Business process reengineering
- Budget and cost management

- SEC reporting and governance
- Merger and acquisition integration
- Financial planning & analysis

PROFESSIONAL EXPERIENCE

Faunton Corporation, Dallas   **2010 to Present**

NASDAQ: FAUN. Global manufacturer of automotive accessories with $X billion in revenue and XX,XXX employees. Acquired by Cormic in 2017.

Divisional Financial Controller—Commercial Products (2014 to Present)
Controller ($XXX million in sales), reporting to president and dotted line to CFO.

Select Achievements
- Oversaw data analysis team in identifying $XX million of revenue leakage.
- Led reengineering projects in Latin America, resulting in $XX million in cost savings.
- Drove implementation of company-wide CRM process.

Director, Planning and Analysis (2010 to 2014)
Created XX-person financial planning and analysis group.

Select Achievements
- Established company-wide strategic planning process, including annual operating plans and quarterly KPIs.
- Evaluated strategic alliances, including 2 completed acquisitions.

Sander and Melbrand, New York   **2003 to 2010**

Preeminent professional services firm (XX,XXX employees globally).

Senior Manager, Professional Services Practice (2009 to 2010)
Advised clients on SEC filing matters and complex accounting issues.

Select Achievements
Finance expert providing advice and due diligence for the $XX billion XYZ-ABC merger.

Senior Audit Manager (2007 to 2009)
Managed a team of audit professionals providing assurance, consulting, and M&A services.

Audit Manager (2005 to 2007)
Led international teams in the global development program, a two-year, international assignment for high-potential leaders, based in Brussels.

Audit Senior (2003 to 2005)
Led teams in performing financial statement audits, IPO preparations, and regulatory filings.

EDUCATION

University of Texas at Austin
B.S., Business Administration and Accounting, 2003

CERTIFICATIONS

CPA, State of Texas (Active License)
Member of the American Institute of Certified Public Accountants

Now, let's examine each component of the resume.

PROFESSIONAL SUMMARY

For someone like Jonathan Sample, whose technical skills speak volumes about his competencies and directly relate to his accomplishments, a "professional summary" is an excellent way to convey information quickly and concisely. For the hiring manager who is glancing at

Jonathan's resume immediately before (and sometimes during) the interview, the professional summary emphasizes meaningful skills and competencies.

As Jonathan's professional summary illustrates (*Example A*), certain words and phrases—strategic planning, cost management, financial planning & analysis—should be used as keywords that relate directly to the skills the company is looking for (as noted in the job description). Whether scanned by a human or a machine, these are the kinds of keywords and phrases that get a candidate noticed. •

A

PROFESSIONAL SUMMARY

Financial executive with extensive experience building and leading teams.
Areas of expertise include:

- Strategic planning
- Business process reengineering
- Budget and cost management

- SEC reporting and governance
- Merger and acquisition integration
- Financial planning & analysis

Who needs a summary?

Mid-level professionals with several years of experience, valuable technical skills, and expertise that directly relates to the contribution they will make to their next employer.

Who doesn't need a summary? Entry-level employees, including recent college graduates and those with only a few years of experience. In most cases, a professional summary would require stretching or inflating what they know or what they've done. It's most important to showcase the experience gained thus far—even if it's only one or two jobs.

C-level executives don't need a summary because, for them, technical skills are assumed—the "table stakes" of their current and next position. C-level executives need to showcase three important aspects of their careers: the size of the companies they've led, the size of the teams they've led, and a pattern of ever-increasing responsibilities.

NO OBJECTIVES, PLEASE!

What you *don't see* in Jonathan's resume (nor in any of the resumes in the Appendix) is an "objective." While many people believe their resume must have one, the problem is that objectives are either "too hot or too cold"—never "just right." They may be too broad or too specific. They can take away from the focus on what benefits you bring or make you seem pigeonholed. To say you're seeking a "challenging team leadership position" might be true, but it says nothing about what you can do for a prospective employer.

For professional-level talent, a summary (as described previously) will suffice. For job-seekers with only a few years of experience, a "headline" is a quick way to make an impact. The headline appears below your name, address, and contact information (never use your work email address). Here are some headline examples:

- **Award-winning graphic designer**
- **Marketing associate with experience running online and social-media campaigns**
- **Communications manager for fast-growing Fortune 1000 company**
- **Biomechanical engineer with nanotechnology expertise**

PROFESSIONAL EXPERIENCE AND ACCOMPLISHMENTS

The **"professional experience"** section is the bulk of your resume. It's a chronological listing (starting with the most recent and working backwards) of *every job* you've had. No gaps! If you've had fifteen jobs in twenty-five years, list them all. The most detail, of course, will be devoted to your current position. In fact, your current job should account for about 75 percent of the detail of your professional experience. The only exception here is if your previous job has significant or different experience that you also want to showcase. If this is the case, you should also highlight your second job.

In this excerpt for Jonathan Sample (*Example B,* page 126), we're looking only at his most recent job, as divisional financial

---

PROFESSIONAL EXPERIENCE

Faunton Corporation, Dallas   **2010 to Present**

NASDAQ: FAUN. Global manufacturer of automotive accessories with $X billion in revenue and XX,XXX employees. Acquired by Cormic in 2017.

Divisional Financial Controller—Commercial Products (2014 to Present)
Controller ($XXX million in sales), reporting to president and dotted line to CFO.

Select Achievements

---

controller for Faunton. Because this company is not a household name, Jonathan has included a brief description of the company and some notable details about it—what it does, its size (revenues and employees), and when it was acquired by a larger firm.

In addition, Jonathan has included a brief summary of his current responsibilities and his contributions (*Example C*) that helped grow

the company. If recruiters or hiring managers read nothing else, they would understand Jonathan's skill set, competencies, and ability to contribute to the next organization.

Jonathan's description (*Example D*, page 127) of his current position at Faunton is brief—just the basic responsibilities and reporting relationships. He uses far more detail to describe his "select achievements." These details showcase his competencies and his ability to contribute to the next employer. In addition, each bullet point contains enough information to be meaningful and to prompt a question from the recruiter or hiring manager.

One way to approach your core accomplishments is to think about *three stories* you will want to tell an interviewer. These stories should quickly capture and convey your technical skills and your leadership capabilities. In other words, these stories should tell what you're good at in a way that will get people to remember you. Your resume will set you up to tell these stories. Each story

> As you draft your core accomplishments, ask yourself, "What am I known for? What are the most important accomplishments I should highlight?"

Divisional Financial Controller—Commercial Products (2014 to Present)
Controller ($XXX million in sales), reporting to president and dotted line to CFO.

Select Achievements
- Oversaw data analysis team in identifying $XX million of revenue leakage.
- Led reengineering projects in Latin America, resulting in $XX million in cost savings.
- Drove implementation of company-wide CRM process.

Director, Planning and Analysis (2010 to 2014)
Created XX-person financial planning and analysis group.

Select Achievements
- Established company-wide strategic planning process, including annual operating plans and quarterly KPIs.
- Evaluated strategic alliances, including 2 completed acquisitions.

You are not a superhero—you did not accomplish everything by yourself. Don't be afraid to credit the team you led or were part of.

should have three parts: the circumstance or challenge, the action taken, and the result.

Be specific with numbers, percentages, and other quantifiable details. If your marketing plan contributed to a 34 percent increase in sales, or if you led a team that improved operational efficiency by 57 percent, say it! Don't worry about the details now—the recruiter or hiring manager who is interested in you will ask those questions during the interview.

Keeping the focus on your story will help you frame your resume for the greatest

impact and prevent you from including unnecessary detail.

And remember, you did not accomplish everything by yourself. You were part of a team, whether as a leader or a member. Saying "we" or "our team" does not dilute your accomplishments; rather, it strengthens your impact. The recruiter or hiring manager reading your resume will know you are truly a team player. It will be far more effective than merely saying "I am a team player." ●

FROM A MILITARY TO A CIVILIAN CAREER

Military veterans are among the highly qualified talent Korn Ferry encounters. Many of them had impressive careers, distinguished by unique leadership assignments and attainment of notable valor. The challenge, though, is that military experiences are often described using a unique vocabulary of titles, responsibilities, and positions. An interviewer who lacks that context may not fully understand or appreciate the scope of a veteran's role and accomplishments. How then, if you're a veteran, can you best convey your military experience in terminology that attracts a civilian employer? There's a practical solution: Develop two resumes.

Following the template in this chapter, develop a resume that uses primarily military terminology to list experiences and contributions. Use minimal civilian language to present missions and accomplishments, but focus on results to showcase technical and leadership capabilities. Then write a second resume, with the same format but with more military-to-civilian translation, so that military assignments are described mostly in civilian terms. For example, instead of using the title "commander," refer to yourself as a "leader."

Which version of your resume is best for the job you're seeking? Ask your network of contacts, your LinkedIn connections, and people in the professional/military organizations you belong to. Identify someone who works at your targeted company. If that person is also a veteran, he or she will more than likely be willing to offer advice on how best to present your military experience in the right context. ●

NO TRANSLATION NECESSARY

If a veteran received an award of valor—such as the Bronze Star Medal for distinguished service—that should be listed in the "profile" section at the top of the resume. This is a powerful validation of the individual's character, sense of purpose, and dedication to the mission. It needs no translation.

THE CREATIVE RESUME

People can get creative with their resumes when the positions they're pursuing require creative skills. (Web designer and graphic artist are just two examples of such positions.) This is not to be confused with a portfolio of work or a video reel, which will be showcased online and sent to potential employers via a link. We're talking here about resumes that are designed and presented to look like everything from movie posters to valentines.

A creative director Korn Ferry works with shared the story of an artist who presented her resume as a piece of art. It was folded into an origami swan and "nested" in a beautifully decorated box. The presentation was so beautiful, it was practically sacrilege to open the resume and destroy the swan. The origami presentation made enough of a statement about the artist's creative vision that she was hired.

It's possible that a creative resume using graphic design, typography, and even humor in unique ways will elevate it (and you) above the rest. But even the most engaging and creative resume still must be concise, accomplishment focused, and readable. Don't allow your design to overshadow your content to the point that it's difficult for anyone to grasp who you are and what you've done. Ask yourself, *Am I showcasing myself—my brand, what I'm known for—in the best way to represent myself, my professionalism, and my accomplishments?*

My advice is to turn to your network and ask how others in your field have designed and presented their resumes to your target companies or similar firms. In addition, you can find plenty of creative-resume examples online. Do a Google search for "creative resumes that got people hired." Above all, make sure that your creative resume conveys a message that will resonate with your prospective employer. ●

YOUR EDUCATION

The longer it's been since you graduated, the farther back your education will be listed. If you are a senior vice president who has worked for several multinational companies, the fact that you went to an Ivy League school is a plus, but it's not the only reason someone should hire you.

For a recent college graduate, the opposite is true. Your education, internships, and significant educational experiences are what you want to showcase. Your resume will probably start with your college education and list internships or other notable experiences at the top. Your job experience (such as summer jobs) will probably be less important in terms of skills, but it should be listed because it shows you have experience in the workplace. ●

How to Sharpen Your Resume

When it comes to resume writing, people procrastinate more than they do with any other task. They dread it. They freeze up. Every time they pick up a pen or sit down at the keyboard, they get writer's block. Here's what I suggest when approaching your resume:

TAKE THE "TV INTERVIEW" APPROACH

In a television interview, a person usually gets no more than twenty to forty seconds to make a point. That's the goal here. Your resume is going to capture the most salient information quickly and concisely.

DO SOME "TIMED" BRAINSTORMING

Stop overthinking! Give yourself a series of timed exercises that will help you get to the most important material—*quickly*. For each of the prompts below, set the timer for two minutes and write five bullet points.

Tell about yourself.

Describe what you've done.

Tell about a time when you overcame a challenge, exceeded your goals, etc.

Describe your five biggest accomplishments.

Identify your two biggest failures.

VIDEO YOURSELF

When you have finished each prompt, take thirty minutes to read, reflect, and revise. Then video record yourself answering each prompt. Your goal is to produce a concise sixty-second answer for each. Revise and record until you are satisfied.

ADAPT YOUR "SCRIPT" TO YOUR RESUME

Using this script outline, begin to write your resume.

FINAL NOTES FOR YOUR RESUME

PROFESSIONAL AFFILIATIONS AND AWARDS

List your association memberships, relevant positions you have held in these organizations, and any honors or awards you have received.

PERSONAL INFORMATION

Some people argue for including personal information; others say you should omit it. My advice is to be strategic about it. Just listing hobbies ("I enjoy reading and gardening") doesn't do much to distinguish you. But activities that say something about your traits should be included: You participate in competitive sports; you've finished multiple Ironman triathlons; you served in the Peace Corps in West Africa; you're an accomplished cellist. If the information showcases a differentiating facet of yourself or what you bring to your next employer, then go for it. International activities (you volunteered at a farm cooperative in South America) can help demonstrate that you have a global perspective.

REFERENCES

It is assumed that you have references, so it's not necessary to list them or say that they are "available upon request."

COVER LETTER

Always write one—even if you're applying online, and it's listed as "optional." A cover letter is an important way to highlight who you are, why you are interested in a position, and why you should be considered for it. A cover letter also personalizes your communication, giving you the opportunity to express yourself as being enthusiastic about exploring this opportunity. In just a few sentences you can translate your background and experience into how you can satisfy the job requirements. •

A LIVING DOCUMENT

A resume is not meant to go back in the mothballs as soon as you land your next job, and then be taken out and dusted off only when you start job-hunting again. Reviewing and revising your resume on an ongoing basis—maybe once a year, whether or not you're "in the market"—will keep this document fresh and relevant. Recording your accomplishments as you achieve them is far easier than trying to remember everything five years later.

But the real living document is the one you present online—often an adaptation of your resume that becomes your LinkedIn profile or other social-media presence. As we'll discuss in the next chapter, managing your social-media presence is an ongoing activity that keeps you relevant and marketable. •

MANAGING YOUR ONLINE PRESENCE

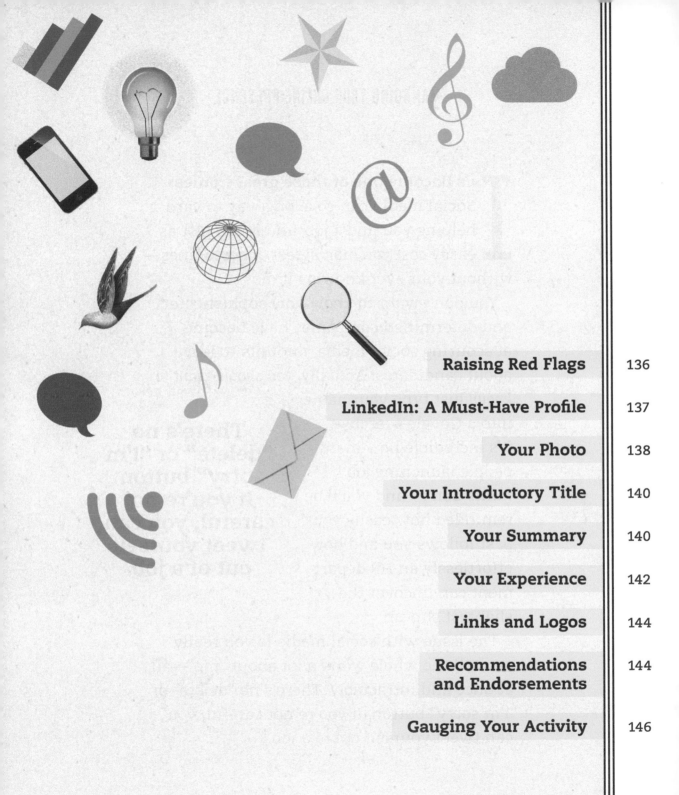

SEVEN

MANAGING YOUR ONLINE PRESENCE

It's become one of those great ironies: Social media can go a long way toward helping you find a job, and it can just as easily cost you many great opportunities— without your ever knowing it did.

You don't want to know how sophisticated and determined companies have become at scouring social-media accounts to learn about candidates. Actually, *you should want to know!* Just type your name into a Google search— it's incredible how many people launching job hunts don't—and you'll be reminded how easily your past follows you and how effortlessly an HR department can uncover the slightest slip-up.

> **There's no "delete" or "I'm sorry" button. If you're not careful, you can tweet yourself out of a job.**

The issue with social media is you really can tell the whole world a lot about "me"—all at once and intractably. There's no "delete" or "I'm sorry" button. If you're not careful, you can tweet yourself out of a job.

Surveys have found that more than half of the companies operating today have rejected candidates because of social media discoveries. I find that employers reject as many as 25 percent of job seekers because of social-media content. The content includes inappropriate photos that typically involve alcohol or other substance consumption, and discriminatory or offensive comments. And almost always when I encounter these candidates, they are so surprised.

"Hey, that was on my 'private,'" said one job candidate who had just learned that she was no longer being considered for a position.

"But you made it public," she was reminded.

What she thought was a "private" social-media post ended up very public—in Google images for all the world to find. It was a photo of the candidate blurry-eyed and scantily clad. She was slouched on an inner tube on a ski slope in the dead of winter, with two dozen purple- and gold-beaded Mardi Gras necklaces around her neck and a Jack Daniels bottle and several Budweiser cans poking out from the snow. The topper, though, was the hand-lettered sign she was holding. It read, "Just another sick day." That was enough for a prospective employer to say, "No thanks."

As she explained, it was a joke. "I wouldn't really do something like that," she said. But the physical world has context; the online world does not. You really should keep private what you do in private, because what "happens in Vegas" doesn't stay there as soon as social media enters the mix.

Older employees tend to think they're safer because they use social media less frequently and may not even have Snapchat or Instagram accounts. But a Google search doesn't discriminate against age, and through LinkedIn, Facebook, and Twitter, seasoned executives have online photos,

---

The Unspoken Truth

✖

What "happens in Vegas" doesn't stay there. If your inappropriate pictures or offensive and discriminatory comments end up online, prospective employers will see them.

posts, and tweets that can present an image that's contrary to the company's goals. Or the online material can be just plain embarrassing.

As I was writing this chapter, a report came out that Harvard University had rescinded admission to at least ten students because of offensive posts in a "private" Facebook chat. Harvard wasn't the first to take such action. A few years ago, another elite private college denied admission to a young student who tweeted derogatory comments about other people *while she was on the campus tour!*

Why would someone be so blatant? It goes back to the false assumption that you've told "only a few people" who are your online friends. But you have, in fact, told the whole world.

People think there is some kind of "wall" between sites such as Facebook, Instagram, and Twitter, and the largely professional ones such as LinkedIn. Your online presence, however, is one entity: your digital brand. ●

RAISING RED FLAGS

An avid basketball fan, Roger followed the sport passionately. Anybody who ever sat courtside heard his profane comments about the coaches, opponents, and refs. Roger also took the same uncensored approach to his tweets—his followers were mostly fanatical fans like him. Within his professional network, of course, Roger presented a different persona. A marketing executive, he was known for being edgy, but most people would describe him as smart, articulate, and funny.

After about five years into his current role, Roger was contacted by a recruiter who had heard him speak about digital marketing during a panel discussion at an industry conference. Intrigued by a new professional opportunity, Roger agreed to a meeting to discuss a chief marketing officer role at a well-established, larger company that wanted someone with digital experience. The firm, though, was known for being somewhat conservative. The CEO's personal values engendered a reserved culture, but it wasn't all buttoned up and stiff, the recruiter assured him.

Before the first interview was arranged, the recruiter called Roger to say he was no longer a candidate for the position. Surprised, Roger asked why. "It's your tweets," the recruiter said. "As soon as the CEO googled you…"

"The CEO?" Roger interrupted.

"Oh, yes," the recruiter said. "He does his own due diligence on candidates. And I'll be honest with you, the language you used in your tweets offended him."

When I spoke with Roger two years later, he was still tweeting about sports, although

> The physical world has context; the virtual world has none. Nothing posted digitally can be deleted, and nothing is private.

without most of the profanity. And he's still in his same job.

These cautionary tales aren't meant to steer you away from social-media. Indeed, it's worth noting that companies also discover a lot of positive traits about candidates online. Just for starters, social-media posts can back up accomplishments and experience the company may not have totally believed. The company may also discover how truly well rounded you are. Perhaps a recruiter will find those Facebook shots of you finishing your third half-marathon, which you trained for while juggling your work and family responsibilities. Creativity—so hard to discover in an interview—may be revealed online, with paintings you did that haven't quite made it to the Louvre but are still impressive. And polished or funny postings can prove you're a great communicator. •

LINKEDIN: A MUST-HAVE PROFILE

But as much as companies may be prying into your Facebook profile or tweets, we all know that the real center of your career brand in the digital world is LinkedIn. Your profile here is where you showcase how you "ACT"—being authentic, making connections, and giving people a taste of who you are.

Consider these numbers: LinkedIn has more than 500 million members worldwide, including executives from every Fortune 500 company. The largest online professional network in the world, LinkedIn is available in more than 24 languages and 200-plus countries. For job seekers, it's a hive of potential recruiter connections and business contacts. People use it as a tool for searching job postings and finding out more about their target companies. And employers and recruiters use LinkedIn to search for and find out more about professionals like you. Hands down, LinkedIn is the most widely used social-media channel for finding job candidates.

But for most people, getting their profile right remains yet another maddening mystery behind job hunting. Naturally, there is no shortage of advice on how to build a LinkedIn profile, including how-to instructions and tutorials on the LinkedIn site. Be careful about some of this advice. I found one nugget that, citing a study, said a closed mouth on a career-site photo is "50 percent less effective" than an open-mouth photo. Of course, I couldn't help thinking about my friends with terrible teeth. Still, our own research and experience suggests that there's a range of strategies, from the simple to the sophisticated, that can help. And certainly, there are some clear pitfalls to avoid. ●

YOUR PHOTO

Who among us thinks they photograph well? The LinkedIn photo is not part of a beauty contest. It's a key component of branding your unique self. Don't forgo a photo and don't alter it. Both send a negative message. The absence of a photo can be interpreted as "I'm too busy to take this seriously." Make sure it's not an old photo, no matter how cool you looked with that '80s punk haircut. Outdated clothes and hairstyles can make you seem irrelevant for the current job market. And of course, if you look one way in a photo and drastically different in person, it creates a concern about authenticity.

What's unfair is you lose points for trying too hard. Dennis, an engineer I know, posted a LinkedIn profile photo taken by a professional studio—with stage makeup and all. He was wearing a suit and smiling

You shouldn't "judge a book by its cover," but everyone does.

and didn't have a hair out of place. Contacted by a recruiter via LinkedIn, Dennis agreed to a phone conversation and then an in-person meeting. There was a Starbucks not far from where Dennis worked, and he arrived early to secure a table for the two of them. When the recruiter arrived, he immediately recognized her from her picture on LinkedIn and waved. But the recruiter walked past him. Stunned, Dennis got up from the table and stopped her before she kept searching through the busy Starbucks to find him.

"Oh, I didn't recognize you," the recruiter said.

No wonder. Dennis looked entirely different. He was bald, and his shirt was unbuttoned far enough to reveal a huge gold chain. He'd even traded his wire-frame glasses for tortoiseshell ones. Awkward!

The often-quoted statistic is that people form an impression about others within seven seconds. But it may be even shorter than that. I read an article about two Princeton psychologists who found that *one-tenth of a second* is enough to form an impression based on a stranger's face. In the psychologists' experiments, people judged traits such as likability, competence, trustworthiness, and aggressiveness in the blink of an eye. That's all it took to form an opinion.

All the details matter. In your LinkedIn photo, you want to appear professional (with some latitude here, depending on your profession) and well groomed—just as you would for a job interview, a client presentation, or a speaking engagement.

Your photo should project confidence and approachability.

FIND A PHOTO YOU LIKE

Use a recent photo you genuinely like, one in which you are smiling naturally and projecting confidence. As long as you're dressed consistently with your professional image, it doesn't matter if the photo is taken in a studio by a professional photographer on your back patio or in your living room by a friend with an iPhone.

ASK FRIENDS TO CRITIQUE THE PHOTO

Once you post the picture, ask a few friends to take a look. Is it clear? In focus? What's the first word that comes to mind when they look at the picture?

TAKE IT TO THE NEXT LEVEL AND SET THE BACKGROUND IMAGE

Your LinkedIn photo is set against a background image. Don't forget this real estate or shrug it off as "window dressing." Here is an opportunity to use your entire profile imagery to project a brand related directly to your business or profession. For recruiters searching through hundreds of LinkedIn profiles, your use of imagery might just be enough to make them stop and say, "This looks interesting." ●

YOUR INTRODUCTORY TITLE

Imagine someone has just asked you, "What do you do?" Your *brief* reply might be, "I'm the vice president of manufacturing for XYZ Global." Or you might say, "I bring next-generation products from design into the marketplace." Both are correct. But which is more effective for you? The answer is, it depends. Here are some considerations:

WHEN YOUR TITLE AND COMPANY SAY IT ALL

If you work for the leader in your field—a Fortune 100 company, the hot digital start-up, a top-tier institution—you may want to showcase your official job title as the introductory title of your LinkedIn profile. Many senior executives of large companies, for example, use their current title and company name. For them, that says it all.

WHEN A FEW DESCRIPTIVE WORDS BROADCAST A BETTER MESSAGE

The other school of thought says to use a *short description* to convey not only what you do, but how you do it: delivering patient-centered health care (versus head of nursing); connecting great people with jobs they love (versus head of talent acquisition); helping people and organizations tell their story and distinguish themselves in the marketplace (versus public-relations professional). Once intrigued, recruiters, hiring managers, and others can glance down a few lines to read your current job title. A word of caution, though: Being creative is not a license to be inauthentic or to stretch the truth. ●

YOUR SUMMARY

This is your "elevator pitch," your sixty-second wrap-up for which LinkedIn allocates 2,000 characters (three to four sentences). Just like an entrepreneur "pitching" a startup, or a writer trying to introduce a screenplay to a producer, you have an idea to sell. That idea is you!

But here's something key to consider: How much pitching will you do? Some people are rewriting their summaries all the time to match particular jobs or job postings. In theory, you could include keywords in your summary to match any posting, then rewrite the summary for the next posting. I think that increases the odds of mistakes, and remember: Each change is broadcast to your connections as an "update." (Some Premier memberships can hide such updates.) Better to go all out writing one summary while keeping these basics in mind:

USE FIRST-PERSON PRONOUNS

It's okay to say "I"—people expect to hear from you directly. Referring to yourself in the third person—"John is an experienced..." "Mary is a talented..."—sounds awkward and undermines the connection you're trying to make.

GO BEYOND THE BUZZ PHRASES AND CLICHÉS

Most people default to the familiar: "I'm a team player." "I collaborate with others." "I'm an effective communicator." That's not a bad place to start. But take it one step further. What does it mean to you to be a team player? "I lead collaborative teams that bring out the best in others and myself to creatively address problems and brainstorm solutions." Use a thesaurus to help you find synonyms that accurately express what you want to say.

MAKE IT MEANINGFUL TO OTHERS

While the *content* of your summary statement makes it all about you, the *connection* it makes is all about others. In a short amount of space and without too many words, you are showcasing who you are and what you bring to your next employer. Keep the audience in mind as you write your summary statement, particularly if you're looking to attract recruiters and hiring managers. ●

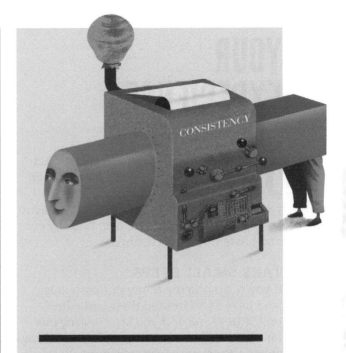

Consistency Matters

With someone's resume in hand, I will typically check it against his or her LinkedIn profile. I'm looking for consistency. Although wording may be different, I want to see the same jobs, titles, and basic information. Gaps, different time frames, and inconsistent information are red flags to me, signaling a problem with either the resume or the way the person is trying to present himself or herself online.

YOUR EXPERIENCE

Just as with your resume, you should use an accomplishment-first approach when presenting your experience in your LinkedIn profile. In fact, a great way to start building your profile is to literally cut and paste from your resume.

TAKE SMALL STEPS

If you're among the many professionals who haven't addressed their LinkedIn profile in years, or if you are creating one for the first time, don't try to do everything at once. Start with what you have. You can leverage your resume to fill out the experience section. Use bullet points to list three to five accomplishments from your current job. Name the accomplishment and the result: "Led a team of twelve colleagues in six countries in launching a new product line that exceeded initial sales projections by 18 percent." For your past jobs, use the same approach, highlighting your top accomplishments.

FOCUS ON THE HOW

Your next revision should move beyond what you accomplished to how you did it. How did you lead that team of twelve colleagues? What were the key points of launching that new product line?

The Importance of "How"

As you explain how you achieved your accomplishments and produced results, you're giving recruiters and prospective employers a look at the value you bring. This is the "taste" that you establish with your "ACT" approach. The more people understand "how" you think, work, and collaborate with others, the more likely your message will resonate with them.

Post videos, blogs, and more. Maybe you participated on a panel at an industry conference or gave a speech on a topic about which you have a great deal of expertise, and the event was recorded and shared online. Or perhaps you wrote a blog about a topic that's meaningful to you, or an article that ran on an industry website. Share these external links that showcase your expertise. They will enliven and enrich your profile. As recruiters look at your LinkedIn presence, you'll instantly distinguish yourself as someone who has a standing in your business or industry.

SHARE CREDIT WITH YOUR TEAM

If you worked on a project with others, tag their names in your LinkedIn post. This is especially important if you're a mid-level manager who directed the team while others did the work. Sharing the credit in no way dilutes recognition of your efforts. On the contrary, you'll showcase yourself as being confident enough in yourself and your abilities to give credit to others. But that's not the only benefit. You now have a "fan base" within your network who are so grateful to be acknowledged that they'll go the extra mile to advocate for you.

UPDATE PERIODICALLY

Just as a photograph from twenty years ago sends a negative message, so does a static LinkedIn profile. As you achieve new accomplishments, add new bullet points and remove older ones. When possible, include links to the product you launched or a presentation you gave. Keep your profile fresh and relevant. By updating your profile, you'll also show the progression in your skills and experiences—and that you're preparing for the next great thing. •

Search Engine Optimization

The summary and experience sections of your LinkedIn profile should incorporate keywords that are relevant to your industry. This will make your profile more effective in terms of search engine optimization, or SEO. Recruiters and hiring managers who search for suitable candidates on LinkedIn are not only looking for people with certain job titles within a particular industry, they are scanning for keywords that indicate your area and level of expertise. One way to identify these keywords is to read job descriptions in your industry and take note of specific qualifications. Then make sure those same phrases are included in your profile in an authentic and meaningful way.

LINKS AND LOGOS

The beauty of an online platform such as LinkedIn is that it allows you to link easily to your current and former employers, as well as to products and even specific projects that you've worked on. For example, let's say you currently work for a well-recognized consumer company. By including the company logo and a link to its LinkedIn page, your profile becomes more visually appealing and more dynamic. Even if a recruiter or hiring manager spends no more than five seconds scanning your LinkedIn profile, a well-recognized logo will make an impact.

But let's say you work for a small startup, one that's not recognizable. When you include a link to that company's LinkedIn page or "About Us" section on its website, you provide an instant resource for a recruiter or hiring manager to find out more about your current employer.

The same goes for the education section of your profile. If your alma mater is a well-known institution, using its logo will leverage the school's "brand recognition." It will also make a visual connection (crucial to your ACT approach) with others who attended that school. You'd be surprised how much weight this carries. Your alma mater also can help when you're networking, including when you want to "pick someone's brain" about a company or industry. If the two of you are alums from the same school, you can take advantage of that commonality and make a connection that increases the chances your email request will be answered.

Finally, links and logos can also enhance the impact of the personal interests that you list in your profile. If you volunteer with Habitat for Humanity, or your first job out of college was with Teach for America, or you had an interesting internship at a well-known nonprofit or institution, that entity's logo and link add visual and dynamic appeal to your profile. •

⫴ RECOMMENDATIONS AND ENDORSEMENTS

LinkedIn's features for collecting recommendations and endorsements can help you build credibility. This is especially true with recommendations and less so with endorsements, which are done literally with the click of a button.

How much thought goes into that? LinkedIn has beefed up its endorsement process by noting when someone who is recognized as being highly skilled in a particular area endorses someone else. For example, your profile might show that in the category of

HOW TO WIN AT LINKEDIN

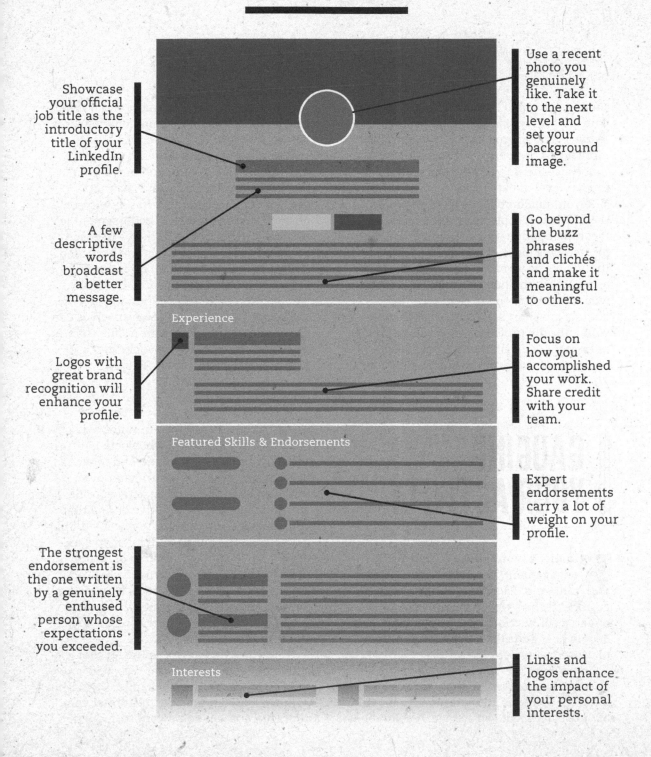

Use a recent photo you genuinely like. Take it to the next level and set your background image.

Showcase your official job title as the introductory title of your LinkedIn profile.

A few descriptive words broadcast a better message.

Go beyond the buzz phrases and clichés and make it meaningful to others.

Experience

Logos with great brand recognition will enhance your profile.

Focus on how you accomplished your work. Share credit with your team.

Featured Skills & Endorsements

Expert endorsements carry a lot of weight on your profile.

The strongest endorsement is the one written by a genuinely enthused person whose expectations you exceeded.

Interests

Links and logos enhance the impact of your personal interests.

social media, Bob Smith and five others who are highly skilled endorse you. Such "expert" endorsements are thought to carry more weight because of the assumption that these are people who can really attest to your level of expertise.

Recommendations are a cut above. In the old days, people asked for a letter of recommendation—a statement typed or printed on a piece of paper that described their value as an employee, their character as a person, and how fortunate an employer would be to hire them. Now recommendations are short statements posted on your LinkedIn profile. Occasionally, a client or former or current colleague will write an unprompted recommendation (for your review and approval). But most of the time, you'll have to ask for recommendations from bosses, mentors, colleagues, and clients.

While many people fall into the quid pro quo of "you recommend me and I'll recommend you," be careful that not every laudatory comment has a twin some place. The most powerful endorsement is the one written by a genuinely enthused person whose expectations you exceeded. It doesn't matter how high up in the organization that person is. A thoughtful, well-written recommendation written by a peer who speaks with some specifics can do more to distinguish your profile than generic comments from people who are many levels above you. •

GAUGING YOUR ACTIVITY

Finally, a word about social-media engagement. As interactive platforms, LinkedIn, Facebook, Twitter, Instagram, and the rest are meant to foster ongoing connections and conversation. People post and share, often on multiple platforms at once.

Just how active you should be on a platform such as LinkedIn is subject to a lot of different opinions and interpretations. One of our social-media strategists recommends being online about fifteen minutes a day, scrolling through to see who posted, hitting "like" or sharing a comment, and maybe posting a comment or two of your own. While you want to keep an active profile, you don't want to be so active online that you make it seem like you're never working.

Recently, the online activity of an executive Korn Ferry was thinking of hiring raised a red flag for me. When I checked out his social-media presence, it appeared he was online multiple times a day, blogging, tweeting, and commenting on anything and everything.

Only you can determine the level of activity that's right for you. Yes, you want to keep abreast of what's happening within your network and to stay in front of your contacts. But you don't want to suddenly

You don't want to be so active online that you make it seem like you're never working.

be seen all over Facebook or LinkedIn. A burst of activity might make others wonder what's up. Did you decide to become very active because you're looking for a job?

Keep in mind that the frequency and relevancy of your posts and comments are leaving a digital footprint. In this world where everything is so transparent and searchable, you want your activity to showcase you as someone who is interested in the world and other people, enthusiastically engaged in your work, and connecting with others in meaningful online conversations. ●

WORKING WITH A RECRUITER

EIGHT

WORKING WITH A RECRUITER

T he email is totally unexpected. As you carefully read it, you can feel your heart racing. You are thrilled! You can't wait to tell your family, and in the meantime, you find yourself whispering to your colleagues— the ones you trust, "You won't believe this, but I just got this email, and..."

It's a new job offer, right? Actually, it's not. The email is from a recruiter. But it certainly has you revved up. Someone you never heard of explains he or she has been studying your qualifications (how nice) and would like to discuss a job opportunity that seems ideal for you (even nicer). Naturally, it pays more than your current job, has better benefits, and is with a great company the recruiter isn't allowed to name.

> ### The Unspoken Truth
>
> ✖
>
> **Being contacted by a recruiter for the first time doesn't mean you're about to get a new job. Working with a recruiter is all about *networking*.**

As the CEO of the world's largest recruiting firm, I can tell you that back in the day, contact from any major recruiter was indeed a good sign. Now, thanks to a new breed of job placers crowding the field, odds are it won't be as big a deal when one reaches out to you.

Granted, it's good news you've been picked, but the news comes with a caveat that too few people appreciate: Recruiters, especially those who work on a contingency basis, cast a wide net, seeking initially to identify as many potential candidates as possible. Dozens and perhaps even a hundred people could be flagged, depending on the level of the position. Numerous candidates could then be contacted, vetted through screenings, and eliminated through interviews and assessments. Clearly, it's a numbers game. For any one job, the math is not working in your favor, especially when you're first contacted through that hope-infusing email.

So you've stopped jumping for joy over the email, and now you may be thinking you should not even reply to it. "I have better things to do," you tell yourself, just like someone else who has received one of these emails might. After all, with the job-hunting process so taxing, who has the time to waste on such a long shot?

But you *should* respond. Very definitely. ●

NETWORKING THE NETWORKERS

Put simply, you shouldn't work with a recruiter to get hired for "a job." Instead, you should be networking with recruiters to increase your chances of being hired at some point for the right job. This requires a shift in your thinking. You want to move away from seeking the instant gratification of getting a new job tomorrow and toward building a long-term relationship with recruiters. You never know: You could be the best candidate for the current job opening, so you absolutely want to respond to the recruiter and learn more about it. But even more important is that this gives you an opportunity to distinguish yourself. Be responsive, professional, and appropriately eager (but never desperate) to hear more.

As with any networking relationship, you shouldn't focus on what the recruiter can do for you right now. It is a process of being introduced, getting to know each other, and staying in touch. As one of Korn Ferry's longtime recruiters suggested, the best time to reach out to a recruiter is when you're already employed and not actively looking for a job. "Careers are long term," the recruiter said. "Don't just call recruiters when your 'hair is on fire' and you need a job."

In fact, 90 percent of the candidates we have placed in jobs—at the senior-executive level with our flagship Executive Search business and at the professional level with our Futurestep business—are "passive candidates."

That is, they were not actively looking for a job before we contacted them. They were engaged in their current positions but were open to having a conversation about a new opportunity.

One early way to work with a recruiter—and foster a long-term relationship that may be fruitful one day—is to help with *his* or *her* searches. If you can't pursue the opportunity you were contacted about, then recommend others who can. And believe me, the recruiter will appreciate the gesture more than you think.

The whole reason recruiters cast such wide nets these days is that companies keep demanding more candidates so that the searches are robust. Considering that kind of strain, it's not surprising that in one survey 65 percent of recruiters said a "talent shortage" was their biggest challenge. So don't be surprised by how grateful a recruiter will be to receive your intel—and how it will make him or her an instant ally of yours. In fact, the recruiters who keep databases of clients—and many do—will likely make a notation after the name of anyone who helped them. •

> Become a resource for recruiters. When you are not the right person for a job, provide other ideas and suggestions. Create a two-way relationship.

GETTING TO KNOW RECRUITERS

One of your career goals should be to get to know the recruiters who specialize in your industry and/or your function. This fact is not well understood: Recruiters specialize by industry (e.g., technology, consumer, retail, financial services, life sciences, etc.)—and by function (marketing, financial officers, human resources, legal, etc.). As with any networking relationship, it is best to be introduced by someone. Ideally, you can be introduced to a recruiter by someone that recruiter has placed. Not only is someone vouching for your credentials, but the recommendation is coming from a successfully placed candidate. Recruiters will check and verify everything about your background. So if you come with the "stamp of approval" from a recruiter who is known in your field and industry, that's a real positive for you.

If this has changed your thinking about working with a recruiter, then good! The best way to work with recruiters is to stop thinking of them like real estate agents, who have listings of multiple houses for sale and are waiting for you to make an offer and move in.

As you build your understanding of how recruiters work, you should understand who the "client" is. Too often, people who are new to the recruiting process hear "client" and think that means candidate—as if the words are synonymous. They're not. If you are under consideration for a job, you are a candidate. The client is always the organization doing the hiring. That's who the recruiter works for—the one who pays for the search.

Recruiters are hired to identify candidates who are best suited to a position. Korn Ferry, for example, is known for its cutting-edge intellectual property in talent assessment. We know how to distinguish great candidates from very good ones.

RECRUITING 101

Recruiters fall into three basic camps according to how they work and the level of talent they specialize in:

CONTINGENCY RECRUITERS

These people work for companies on a contingency basis. That is, they get paid only if one of the candidates they identify is hired. So contingency recruiters have a big incentive to cast a wide net and identify a large number of potential candidates. (This also explains why they're sometimes referred to as "headhunters.") Among contingency recruiters is a subgroup of mostly junior people, who are typically tasked with searching online to identify potential candidates who will then be passed along to more senior recruiters. Once a large pool is selected, the people in it are evaluated, and a smaller number of suitable candidates are passed along to the employer.

If you make less than $100,000, most likely the recruiter who contacts you is working on a contingency basis. These recruiters' need to identify good candidates creates an opportunity for networking. Always be responsive to a recruiter's email or call. Over time, keep the recruiter informed of job changes and promotions, so your information is up to date.

INTERNAL RECRUITERS

Companies have internal recruiters who are often paid a salary but may receive a bonus for successfully bringing in talent. Internal recruiters may work with external recruiters to

> **Recruiters aren't like real estate agents with multiple listings. Recruiters are hired by companies to staff specific positions.**

How to Get Recruiters' Attention

Respond when you receive an email or call.

Reach out to recruiters who work in your sector and at your level.

Maintain ongoing relationships.

source talent for a specific job. When dealing with an internal recruiter, be sure you treat him or her the way you would the hiring manager.

RETAINED RECRUITERS

When a company needs to find top talent to fill a position, such as one on its leadership team, it will turn to Korn Ferry or another executive-search firm. The firm is paid a retainer fee (hence, the term "retained recruiter") for conducting the search, even if the company ends up hiring someone not identified by the recruiter, such as an internal candidate who is promoted. On average, Korn Ferry undertakes 5,000 executive searches a year. In addition, our Futurestep division, which engages in talent searches at the professional level, makes more than 40,000 placements a year.

Retained firms typically do searches for only seasoned professionals. For senior executives, that means those making a minimum of $250,000 a year in salary and bonuses. The five largest retained search firms by revenue (as rated by Hunt Scanlon) are:

Korn Ferry
Spencer Stuart
Egon Zehnder
Heidrick & Struggles
Russell Reynolds

In addition to these firms are many specialty outfits focused on specific industries or positions. Combined, these firms might conduct more than 20,000 executive searches a year. But the number of potential candidates can be in the millions. Think about how many executives there are in the business world—in companies large and small, public and private. Even for a specific function such as chief financial officer, there could be hundreds of thousands of potential executives, including internal candidates. No matter how you figure it, the number of available candidates is many times greater than the number of job openings. Each vacant position also has its own requirements. CFOs, for example, are specialized not only by their function, but also by their industry. This narrows the potential opportunities for candidates even more.

The search process has changed for the candidate and the company over the past couple of decades. Before the Internet, the available talent pool was smaller. In fact, an executive who knew three or four recruiters could almost be assured of receiving a plethora of job offers. Today, the candidate pool is larger because technology has enabled recruiters to identify more talent in more locations. In addition, people are generally more mobile than in the past, which means that for the right opportunity,

It's All about the Fit

Recruiters are in the business of connecting companies with the best candidates. To do that, they must have in-depth knowledge of specific candidate pools. An example of such a pool is the one for retail chief information officers in the United States. Making a successful placement depends on knowing the candidates and determining which are best suited to a position and the hiring company's culture, mission, and purpose. It's all about the fit.

location is not a limiting factor.

With more potential candidates to choose from, companies can be more specific about their requirements: the number of companies someone has worked for, the size of the teams he or she has managed, and the laundry list of desired capabilities and experiences. For example, a company may have ten "must-haves" for an experienced position such as senior vice president. Twenty years ago, a good candidate who had three out of ten qualifications would probably be acceptable to an employer, with the expectation that the executive could learn and master the other seven. Today, however, an employer will probably hold out until it finds someone who possesses all ten qualifications—or as many as possible, depending on competition for talent in a particular field or function.

To fulfill clients' hiring needs, Korn Ferry consultants develop and maintain deep networks of candidates, and take pride in knowing the best talent in various industries and functions. Our specialty practices cover advanced technology, consumer, finance, health care and life sciences, professional services, boards of directors, energy, industrial, private equity, associations, education, and not-for-profit. We have nearly 8,000 employees worldwide working out of approximately 100 offices in

50 countries. Drawing from our extensive talent database, we act as "matchmakers" between the hiring organization (our client) looking to fill a specific role and executives who are well suited to the job. We use sophisticated assessments of a candidate's knowledge, experience, temperament, and other traits to determine if he or she is the best fit. With a wealth of assessment data, we like to say that we know executives even better than they know themselves.

Once candidates are chosen, here's how the process might go, depending on the job and the number of candidates who could be a finalist for it:

THE FIRST CUT

Initial vetting might reduce the number of candidates from hundreds to fewer than twenty who could be a good fit for the role and the company.

THE SECOND CUT

Further vetting could cut the list of candidates in half. This vetting process will likely include assessments and interviewing, as well as other steps.

THE RECOMMENDATION

The recruiter will recommend to the company a handful of candidates. The company will review the recommendations and bring in the candidates it wants to meet in person. If the company does not accept any of the candidates, or if the job qualifications have changed or been refined, the recruiter will go back to the talent pool. ●

EVERYTHING YOU WANTED TO KNOW ABOUT RECRUITING, BUT WERE AFRAID TO ASK.

DEFINE OBJECTIVES & SPECIFICATIONS

Analysis of client's business culture

Develop position scope and responsibilities, compensation package, reporting relationships, and the profile of the desired executive

Develop the search plan

IDENTIFY CANDIDATES

Identify and confirm target sources using proprietary database and network of contacts

Identify candidates, including internal ones as appropriate

Screen and evaluate candidates

Prepare background profiles

Review profiles with client

THE DOS AND DON'TS OF WORKING WITH A RECRUITER

Without question, a good working relationship with a recruiter can help take your career to the next level. I asked Korn Ferry's recruiters for their thoughts on how to establish and develop that relationship. I also asked them to reflect on their experiences—positive

and negative—with job candidates. Not surprisingly, most of their advice falls into the "ACT" category:

BE AUTHENTIC

Be honest and transparent about who you are, your background, your current job and responsibilities, and your current compensation. Never lie or exaggerate. For example, don't lead the recruiter to believe that you've just been promoted from senior director to vice president, when in fact that hasn't happened yet (other than in your wishful thinking). Don't inflate your salary. If you think you're underpaid, then say so: "I believe I'm under-market, but I'm currently making X per year." And if you've left your last position, tell the recruiter. Don't pretend that you're still there. Recruiters check everything!

SEARCH ASSESSMENT

Develop profile for the position with the client

Conduct online candidate assessments

Compare candidate results to profile

INTERVIEWS

Facilitate client interviews of candidates

Obtain client and candidate feedback

Conduct reference checks

Prepare detailed profiles and evaluation reports on each candidate's strengths and weaknesses

Select finalists to be interviewed

SELECT CANDIDATE

Conduct finalists interviews

Negotiate salary and benefits

FOLLOW-UP

Create smooth transition, including onboarding and development plan

A good working relationship with a recruiter can help take your career to the next level.

CONNECT

When a recruiter reaches out to you, return calls and emails, even if you're not actively looking for a job. If you are initiating contact, use LinkedIn or a firm's website to identify a recruiter who specializes in your area. Send a concise email that explains in the first two sentences who you are and what you do. Tell the recruiter that you'd like to get on his or her radar, and attach your resume.

Don't blast emails to every recruiter you find on a website such as Korn Ferry's. If you send your "I'd like to introduce myself" email, complete with a resume, to two dozen people in the company, hoping to hit the right one, it will backfire. Most of the recruiters you reach will not specialize in your industry sector or function. When they forward your email to the right colleague, that person is going to receive numerous identical emails from you. What does that say about you and your lack of preparation?

Do your homework. Find the recruiter who specializes in your industry sector or function. Better yet, reach out to your network to see if you can get a warm introduction to that person.

From there, it's a matter of giving the recruiter a feel for who you are. Be focused, interested, and confident. And remember the likability factor: We all prefer to work with people we like. If a recruiter is going to put you in front of a client, he or she wants to be confident of your people skills. And when a recruiter meets with

OH, THE THINGS PEOPLE SAY...

A consultant working on a large assignment to staff a call center asked a routine question as part of the initial interviews: "Can you tell me about a challenging situation that you've faced?" One candidate's answer, though, was anything but routine. "I'd have to say the most challenging situation I faced was when my boyfriend broke up with me and started dating my mother."

Another recruiter, screening candidates for a mid-level position, asked about a position listed on the person's resume. "I took that job early in my career, and it worked out very well for me," the candidate said. "I was a caregiver for an elderly person who changed his will and left all his money to me."

"...the most challenging situation I faced was when my boyfriend broke up with me and started dating my mother."

you, he or she will want to see how polished and professional you are.

As you progress through the search process, stay in touch with the recruiter. Your experience and feedback are very important, particularly if you become a finalist or are placed in the job. Another Korn Ferry recruiter had this advice for candidates as they progress through the interviewing process with the hiring organization: "Your feedback is very important. We need to communicate it back to the client. And please, don't ignore follow-up calls for feedback during your first year. Instead, think about cultivating your relationship with the recruiter and honoring the work of the team who helped you land your new job."

Equally important to your relationship with a recruiter is what you don't do. If you make a bad impression with a recruiter, that red flag will follow you. People's memories are long, and recruiters keep databases on every client and candidate with whom they have contact. Common sense, good manners, and professionalism go a long way. At all costs, avoid doing anything that will hurt your relationship with a recruiter.

DON'T AMBUSH

This one is really a pet peeve for recruiters: Picture a purely social occasion—a dinner party, graduation, wedding, or other non-professional event. As part of the casual conversation, the question is asked, "What do you do for a living?" When someone says, "I'm a recruiter," it's suddenly open season on that person, regardless of the setting. Recruiters want to be helpful,

and they do want to meet good candidates. That's their job. But they will tell stories of hiding in corners to avoid ambushes by people who don't understand how the recruiting process works and who insist, "You *must* have a job for me!" Some would rather identify themselves as experts in rare communicable diseases than to have to tell people at a social occasion, "No, I'm sorry, but I cannot help your (spouse, child, friend, cousin) who has been out of work for a year and is looking for a job in a field that I don't specialize in. I don't have a list of jobs in my back pocket."

So what should you do when the parent next to you at the Little League game or the passenger seated beside you on the plane turns out to be a recruiter? *Don't think about yourself!* Treat recruiters like you would anyone else. People like to talk about themselves. Ask what they like about their job. What are some of the more interesting or challenging placements they've made? By the end of the conversation, that parent or plane passenger probably will ask *you* for your card. If the recruiter doesn't work in your field, you can be almost sure that he or she will make a warm introduction to a recruiting colleague who does. That's effective networking in action!

DON'T PLAY GAMES

It's a big offense to not tell the recruiter that you're involved in other searches. It's okay to be an active candidate, pursuing multiple opportunities, but let the recruiter know. If you are a finalist in another search, tell the recruiter. His or her client may speed up its process so that it has the chance to make

What Were They Thinking?

The candidate who, in the middle of the interview with the client, asked for the WiFi password so he could download a movie for the flight home.

The candidate who ate a bowl of cereal during a Skype interview with a client. (It's hard to sound articulate and knowledgeable while crunching Raisin Bran.)

The candidate who didn't tell her spouse that the interview was by Skype, not phone, and he walked by in the background—right out of the shower and without wearing a towel.

---

you an offer. Blindsiding a recruiter with another opportunity, though, will kill your current and future chances.

We have some memorable war stories concerning candidates who didn't disclose concurrent job searches. There's the one about the guy who went all the way through the interview process and accepted the offer. But the first day on the job came and went without the candidate's showing up for work, calling, or returning any of the messages left by the internal recruiter. Finally, at the end of the day, he contacted the company. He had simultaneously accepted a job with another firm and went to work there for one day—just to test it out. Needless to say, he lost his chance of ever being hired for another job by the company.

Then there was the candidate who became the top finalist for a position but never disclosed a personal situation that, in the end, precluded him from accepting an offer. (He had to take a leave of absence to care for an ill family member.) If only the candidate had let the recruiter and the employer know what was going on, they would have been accommodating. Instead, everyone was left scrambling because the candidate unexpectedly withdrew from the process. (This is a reason why—just in case—recruiters identify two or three final-ists, not just one.)

DON'T BE DESPERATE

Whether you have connected with a recruiter on LinkedIn, sent an email inquiry, or received an outreach, don't appear desperate. The analogy to dating is unavoidable. Yes, be responsive and enthusiastic, prompt and professional in your follow-up. Send "thank you for your time and interest" emails, and follow up with questions. Be available for interviews, by phone with the recruiter and in person with the company if you make the cut of viable candidates. But too much contact with the recruiter spells desperation. The recruiter can't help but wonder, *Is this person about to be fired? What's going on that this person suddenly can't wait to change jobs?* And never voice your anxiety about getting a job. The recruiter isn't your therapist or your best friend. It's a professional relationship.

The bottom line is, as your career advances, recruiters will want to meet you. When you reach the appropriate career level, you should absolutely get yourself on the radar of a top recruiter who does retained searches. At any level, though, a relationship with a recruiter can be productive for both of you. But you have to be patient. Know how the field works—and the value of being a "passive candidate." Stay on a recruiter's radar the right way, and you may well be guided to the landing you always wanted. ●

YOUR INTERVIEW PREP:
DON'T PSYCH YOURSELF OUT!

NINE

YOUR INTERVIEW PREP: DON'T PSYCH YOURSELF OUT!

You're driving to work when suddenly you notice in your rearview mirror the dreaded red and blue flashing lights. "Maybe I was going five miles per hour over the speed limit," you tell yourself. Or was it ten? The voice of authority booms, "Pull over to the side of the road." Your body goes through a series of involuntary responses: Your stomach churns; your mouth becomes dry; you sweat profusely.

Welcome to what it can feel like when you're interviewing for a job.

A job interview has been described as a cross between a trip to Disneyland and a visit to the dentist...

A job interview has been described as a cross between a trip to Disneyland and a visit to the dentist to have your wisdom teeth extracted: While looking forward to it, you also dread it, fearing it will be as bad as when the dentist peers into the farthest reaches of your gum line and calmly says, "You might feel a pinch" (which we all know is code for "This is going to hurt like hell").

My advice is to stop thinking about speeding tickets and wisdom teeth! If you let your imagination run wild, you're going to psych yourself out. You'll amp up your panic until you freeze, unable to put two coherent sentences together, or you overcompensate by talking nonstop.

That's clearly what was happening to the man I saw recently at the corner table in a Starbucks. His leg was pumping up and down as he shuffled through notecards. I could see his resume on the tabletop from where I was standing.

"Job interview, huh?" I said as I approached him.

He looked up, his eyes intense with caffeine and desperation. "Yeah, and I really need this job."

"Well, you're not doing yourself any favors," I told him, pointing to his triple red eye (coffee with three shots of espresso). "The

first thing you need to do is take some deep breaths and *relax*. If you go into the interview looking like this, you're going to blow it."

Now I had his attention.

Memorizing his resume like it was a script was a waste of time. He wasn't auditioning for *Annie*! Instead he had to ACT, which I explained quickly to him: being authentic, making a connection, and giving people a taste of what it's like to work with him.

"Your goal is to have a conversation with your interviewer, not an interrogation," I told him. "Don't treat this like somebody is going to shine a light in your eyes and ask you tough questions! This is a conversation, pure and simple."

Then I asked him if he had a picture on his phone that was special to him.

"My family," he said, showing me the screen. "That's what matters most—not this job

---

The Unspoken Truth

✖

The stupidest, most obvious things can derail your interview. Don't be the guy with the two odd socks! You make one easily avoidable mistake, and everything unravels.

interview," I told him. "Think about two hours from now, when the interview is over and you're going home to see your family. You keep them in mind, and you'll have a great interview."

And then I wished him good luck.

No matter if this is your first or second professional job out of college, or you're a senior executive who has been through the drill countless times, your emotions are bound to be mixed and intense—like the guy at Starbucks was experiencing. This is exactly what you've been waiting for. Finally, you have an interview with a company you really want to work for, and you'll be speaking—by phone or video or in person—with someone who could very well be your next boss.

The standard wisdom, as presented in most career books, is to prepare for the interview by scripting and rehearsing what you're going to say. Well, not so fast. While you should know your "lines," learning them is not the first thing you should do. Before you get to what you want to say, be sure you have a strategy—a game plan—centered on ACT. That's what this chapter is all about. •

NOBODY GETS OUT OF SIXTH GRADE

Before diving into your preparation, you want to recognize what makes the interview process so difficult. Although you may have some preconceived ideas, you really don't know what you're going to be asked, or whether the interviewer is going to be more like the cop who pulled you over or your favorite grade-school teacher. You're also facing the unknown of who you are up against— whether you're the favorite candidate or someone who barely made the cut. And then there's the more psychologically complex issue of your not being able to control the process. Yes, all these factors certainly play a part. But for most people, a deeper emotional current runs through the entire interview process: We never really get out of sixth grade.

Think about it. Back when you were eleven or twelve years old, the biggest worries on your mind were:

Are the other kids going to like me?

Will they want me on the team?

Will they share what they know/have?

Will they help me win, or will they undermine me?

Now tell me, which one of these concerns *doesn't* apply to the interview process? For a lot of people, looking at an interview this way is an eye-opener that helps them make sense of their feelings. Their "aha moment" comes when they realize that going for the interview, while an exciting step, makes them uncomfortable because they feel so vulnerable.

All the unknowns and emotional triggers surrounding your job interview come down to the fact that we never get out of sixth grade.

It doesn't take a psychologist to know that these adult feelings can have deep roots in childhood experiences. It's not our purpose here to untangle complex emotions and identify old triggers. Rather, it's enough to recognize that what you feel in an interview is, at the most fundamental level, the same way you felt in sixth grade. You want to be accepted, to be picked for the team, and to win. And most fundamental of all, you want people to like you.

You increase your chances of being liked and accepted with the way you ACT (authentic, connection, taste of how you are to work with). ●

Inside the Interviewer's Head

With more than a half-century in the "people" business, we at Korn Ferry can speak with some knowledge about what's going on in an interviewer's head during the whole "chat." Here are some of the thought processes and how to deal with them:

TAKE A NUMBER

The HR official may have already seen seven other people that morning when you come in all cheerful and ready. Take a moment to read his or her body language and face—especially the eyes. Is this someone ready to match your excitement, or is he or she tired or bored? Then take it from there.

YOUR WEEKEND BORES ME

No, the interviewer isn't waiting all morning to hear how a total stranger washed his car on Sunday. But good interviewers are trained to put candidates at ease, to elicit honest answers. So idle open questions are part of the process.

"I DON'T KNOW"

It's a phrase we are taught never to say. But a good interviewer will appreciate its honesty in the right place. It's better than hearing a long-winded effort to talk around a subject you're clueless about.

POWER PLAY

As a rule, hiring managers understand the pressure you are under, but they face enormous pressure to hire well. They need to be in control, which means you need to answer their questions as directly as possible, and know when to…

PLEASE, GET OUT!

That's putting it harshly, but interviewers generally allocate their time carefully. So try to mimic all "wrapping-up" movements; candidate No. 9 (for that day!) is sitting outside.

MAKING THE MOST OF
THE FIRST SEVEN SECONDS

It's a statistic you've probably heard quoted frequently: It takes people only seven seconds to make a judgment about others. During that very short time, an interviewer will make crucial determinations about you, including your likability, your trustworthiness, how aggressive or passive you seem, and how well you would fit in with others on the team. There's actually a science that explains this phenomenon (and no doubt one of the leading minds from the Korn Ferry Institute could give the details), but it's helpful to know that meeting people activates the part of the brain we use to assign value to people (and objects)—essentially split-second judgments of their importance to our social world.

Based on this initial determination (typically unconscious), your interviewer will decide (probably also unconsciously) whether to help you in the interview—by rephrasing questions, giving helpful feedback, assuring you with verbal and nonverbal cues—or to interrogate you. Therefore, much of what we address in this chapter is about making those *seven seconds* productive. With so much riding on this all-important first impression, you can't leave it to chance. You must prepare.

You also can't underestimate the importance of the seemingly superficial things that influence a first impression. There are several items you need to address in the days and weeks before the interview. Don't leave these details to the last minute or the morning of the interview. You'll have enough on your mind that day!

And that's just part of what can go wrong. The truth is that smart people and even seasoned professionals can do some very dumb things. Unfortunately, the competition among experienced and talented professionals is so intense that one of these "sins" can put an end to a promising opportunity.

At all cost, avoid the Twelve Deadly Sins of Interviewing. •

> No matter how many interviews you've been on, or how well you think on your feet, you must prepare so that you can ACT your best—being authentic, making a connection, and giving others a taste of what it's like to work with you.

THE TWELVE DEADLY SINS OF INTERVIEWING

THE FIRST SIN
LYING, EXAGGERATING, OR INFLATING

You can never recover from a lie. You tell the recruiter and the hiring manager that you're still working at your last job, though you've already quit, or you were fired. You want to appear more desirable as a candidate so you make it seem like you're still at that company. What's the harm? After all, you *did* work there. Big mistake! You have to tell the truth. *Period.* Even CEOs have been fired; it's not the end of the world. Someone will verify the facts of what you say. This is not the time to rewrite history. If you do, it's game over.

I'll never forget the story told by someone who worked for me. My guy, let's call him "John," was interviewing a candidate who, as it turned out, went to John's alma mater. John asked the candidate, "Were you in a club or a frat?" The candidate said, "Frat." John, of course, asked which one. When the candidate said the name of the frat, John replied, "Really? Me, too." Then John reached over to give him the frat's secret handshake. The candidate didn't know what to do. He fumbled, trying to follow along, then dropped his hand to his lap. "You weren't in that fraternity, were you?" John said.

"Nope," the candidate answered. "I guess the interview is over."

"Yes," John said. "It is."

Once you lie, exaggerate, or inflate, then *everything* you say or have said becomes suspect. And if you think no one will find out, trust me, someone will.

One of my colleagues recalled an experience from earlier in his career, when he was conducting on-campus interviews with college students. One resume stood out in his mind, because this student stated that he was proficient in Kiikaonde, a dialect spoken in central Africa. As it turned out, this recruiter

---

Truth Is Stranger Than...

Another colleague shared this story: "An internal candidate submitted his resume for a job. As I read his current job responsibilities, I thought, *Gee, this wording looks awfully familiar.* Then it dawned on me: He had cut and pasted a job description from the company intranet—a job description I had written. I was reading my own words! To make matters worse, this internal candidate was in an entry-level position and had culled wording from a description for the corporate lawyer."

also speaks Kiikaonde. When the candidate arrived for their meeting, the recruiter greeted him warmly in Kiikaonde. No response. The recruiter tried again, more slowly this time—just a simple greeting. Still no response.

"I take it you're not proficient in Kiikaonde," the recruiter said.

"No," the student said. "I took this two-day seminar. We learned a few words..."

Lying not only casts doubts on who you are, it is also disrespectful to the interviewer, who probably feels a little tricked by you. Be authentic! People want to know who you are, not discover who you aren't.

THE SECOND SIN
DRESSING LIKE YOU'RE APPEARING ON *DANCING WITH THE STARS*

Too tight, too clingy, too low-cut, too short, too casual. We've seen it all—on both men and women. Granted, not every job interview requires a suit, but you still should present yourself as well groomed and professional. Know the difference between business professional (you'll need to wear a suit—jackets for men and women) and business casual (well groomed, but take it down one notch). When in doubt, ask your network for advice.

While an interview is not a beauty contest, appearance does matter. Plan your outfit ahead of time. Try it on. Make sure

it's clean, pressed, and still fits. The last thing you want is a "wardrobe malfunction" during your interview. The hemline that's not sewn in and starts to sag as you walk into the office lobby or the suit jacket that's too tight to button—suddenly this becomes all you can think about. Or before the interview begins, you notice that one of your socks is black and the other is blue, and you consciously start to hide your ankles.

You don't need to show up in designer clothes, but you should wear professional attire that's on par with or a step above the environment in which you are going to work. This means doing your homework ahead of time.

One of my colleagues at Korn Ferry tells the story of interviewing a high-level candidate who came to the meeting disheveled—clothes wrinkled, hair barely combed. As my colleague recalled, "I said to myself, a job interview should be the best hour of someone's professional life. If this is the best that this guy's got, it isn't saying much."

Ask people in your network who work or used to work at the company where you're interviewing about the norm for dress in the office. What's considered appropriate? Sometimes the internal recruiter or HR person arranging the interview will tell you.

You don't want to show up at a jeans-and-hoodie tech firm dressed like you're going to a wedding or a funeral. You'll appear out of sync with the environment or even irrelevant. And you don't want to go to a bank or an investment firm looking like you're meeting a friend for a casual lunch.

Granted, we all have our own sense of style, and dressing is one way we express our

YOUR PROFESSIONAL-APPEARANCE COUNTDOWN

A week before

Pick out your interview outfit. Try it on. Make sure everything is clean, pressed, fits well—and matches. You'll probably sit next to your interviewer, so pay attention to your socks and the length of your pants or skirt.

Three days before

Address the smaller details such as your shoes—polished, no scuffs.

The day of the interview

Do a "mirror check" before you leave for the interview. Check your fingernails (no dirt), your teeth, and your face. Always do a second check in the office restroom after you arrive. Anything stuck in your teeth? Breath fresh? Use the bathroom.

On the way to the interview

Do not buy or bring anything that could spill on you. Just ask the guy who flew from Chicago to New York the morning of his interview. He ordered tomato juice; there was turbulence. Get the picture? And if you are flying in for an interview, never check your suitcase. A lost suitcase can mean an expensive shopping trip when you land.

individuality. But how much of a statement do you really want to make, presuming that you want to be considered for the job?

My twenty-four-year-old daughter has a very small nose ring. I've told her many times that she should remove it, especially when she has a job interview. One Sunday night, a mere fourteen hours before her interview on Monday morning, she called to tell me she could not get her nose ring out. My wife and I were frantic. Should we pick her up and take her to the emergency room? What about a tattoo parlor or a piercing shop?

As we raced for answers, our daughter asserted that she has the right to be herself. How can she be authentic if she changes her appearance? She did have a point. But as I explained, a nose ring is an optional accessory; therefore, she needs to think about whether to wear it. People are going to have initial impressions and form opinions, positive or negative, based on that nose ring.

My daughter went online to check out the company's website and its Facebook page, and called someone she knew at the company. It was a "salad Wednesday" (communal lunch) and "take your pet to work" kind of a place. So, she left the nose ring in. She got the job, and now she brings her dog to work.

Your appearance—your grooming, your hair, your tattoos (whether you show or cover them)—does say a lot about you. But it's not really about you! Remember your ACT. You're trying to connect with others. You want to appear relatable so you can have a meaningful conversation. It's up to you to figure out, based on your "audience,"

You don't want to show up at a jeans-and-hoodie tech firm dressed like you're going to a wedding or a funeral.

how to best present yourself. You want to broadcast, "I can work here. I fit; I belong."

And speaking of "fit," we still talk about "Stapler Man." In fact, he's a bit of a legend.

Dressed in his best Canali suit, a candidate came to our office to meet with me. Unfortunately, he must have purchased the suit a while ago and hadn't tried it on lately, because it looked like it was one size too small. Maybe he didn't have another suit to wear or enough time to change. Whatever the reason, he wore that straining Canali to the interview.

Everything was okay when he arrived at the reception desk fifteen minutes early. Then just as he started to take a seat in the waiting area, there was the sound of tearing fabric. A moment later, he reappeared at the reception desk. "Do you have a stapler?" he asked.

The receptionist accommodated his request, and the man disappeared with the stapler. Then, from a small unoccupied conference room, came a "click, click, click…" sound.

When I came to the reception area to greet the man, I was surprised to see him emerging from the conference room with a stapler in his hand. His face was flushed, and his shirt looked damp. When he sat down in my office, very slowly, it dawned on me what had happened. If nothing else, he certainly was ingenious. And I had to admire his poise under pressure.

As it turned out, the position wasn't right for him. I did recommend him to a firm that was looking for someone with his skill set, but among the small circle of us who remember, he'll forever be Stapler Man.

The moral of the story is, know what you're going to wear well ahead of time. Try it on a week before the interview (in case you have to go shopping) and again the night before. You must make sure it fits, so you can fit in. Finally, when in doubt, dress up.

THE THIRD SIN
ARRIVING LATE

Given the importance of an interview, you'd think that people would be ready to go—practically pacing in the parking lot, waiting for the moment when they can enter the building and show their stuff. Don't be one of those hapless candidates who shows up late because you got lost or underestimated the travel time. You don't want the very first thing you say to the hiring manager to be "I'm sorry I'm late," as you offer your sweaty hand to shake.

Being punctual is a deal-or-no-deal situation. Arriving late is not only rude to those you've kept waiting, it is also highly unprofessional and counters your ACT objective of giving people a taste of what it would be like to work with you. If you're late, you're telling others that you are unreliable.

If your interview is in another city or state, fly in the night before. If you must drive a long distance, leave extra early. Even if the interview is in the same city where you now work, you still have to prepare. Practice driving the route from your home or current office to the interview site so you know where to go. Account for traffic and the unexpected.

If you are late for the interview, you have probably just lost the job.

Plan to be on site or in the neighborhood one hour before the interview. No, you're not going into the office at that time. Arriving too early makes you appear amateurish and desperate. It broadcasts, "Please hire me. I need this job." You're going to spend most of that hour in your parked car or in a coffee shop around the corner. Do some visualizations of your ACT. Meditate on what is meaningful to you so you can keep your perspective. Leave your car so that you are in the office ten or fifteen minutes ahead of time.

Keeping It in Perspective

Being asked to interview at a company is an important milestone in your job search. It could be even bigger than that. Maybe you're interviewing for a position you really want at a company you greatly admire. This would be your dream job!

All that may be true, but you must keep things in perspective. While you want to make a great impression—showcasing your strengths, highlighting your accomplishments, demonstrating how you can make a difference to the organization—you can't go into the interview thinking this is a "life or death" moment. If you carry that feeling into the interview, you're going to radiate anxiety and desperation.

As hard as it may be, you need to detach a little. One way is to give yourself a visual of what's important in your life. Put a picture on your phone of someone special, your pet, a place you like to visit, or an activity you enjoy. Or carry a small inspiring photo in your pocket. As you prepare for the interview, use that picture or photo to remind yourself of the good things you have in your life right now. As you sit in your car or in the coffee shop before the interview, let that image soak in and calm you down. This is what grounds you in life and reminds you that you are not your job. Your title and salary do not define you. The quality of your life, the meaningfulness of your relationships, the way others feel about you and you feel about them—these are the things that are most important.

THE FOURTH SIN
NOT DOING YOUR HOMEWORK

People miss this one all the time. They go into an interview without knowing much about what a company does. Or else they get confused momentarily between this interview and the one two days from now. Whatever the cause of confusion, if you commit this "sin," it will become painfully obvious to all involved that you don't know much about the company. Case in point: When the hiring manager mentions "Joe Smith," a look of confusion crosses your face and you ask, "Who is that, exactly?" Not a smart move. The hiring manager replies, "Our CEO."

Learn all you can about the company— its leadership team, its current successes and challenges, its history. If possible, get some firsthand experience with the company's products and services: Buy them; try them; talk to people who use them. And use your head in the interview. If you're meeting with PepsiCo and you're offered a beverage, don't ask for a Coke. The all-time blooper was committed by a candidate interviewing with a senior executive of a well-known fast-food chain. Halfway through the discussion, the candidate leaned over and said, "Be honest with me: You don't eat this crap, right?"

Greater knowledge about the company, its products and services, and its customers will also help you present your skills and experiences in context. You'll appear more relevant to the hiring manager. And the more relevant you are, the better the connection you'll make.

Don't Leave Home Without ...

Copies of your resume ✓

A reference list ✓

A notepad and a ✓
pen that works

Breath mints (not gum!) ✓

A Band-Aid ✓

Tissues ✓

But Never Bring Along ...

Your Mother.

I've heard countless stories of moms scheduling interviews, showing up for interviews, and doing the follow-ups personally. It doesn't stop there. Several years ago, we had to let a number of people go. The mother of one of these individuals called to protest: Surely we had made a mistake. Her son was a hard worker, a great person, did so well in school...

Cut the apron strings! Otherwise it's the mother of sudden death for your opportunity.

THE FIFTH SIN
NOT KNOWING WHO YOU ARE GOING TO MEET

You receive an email from a recruiter, human resources, or the hiring manager with the details of the time and place for your meeting. But you never google the person who is going to interview you or look at his or her LinkedIn profile. If you had done so before your interview, you wouldn't try to break the ice by asking, "So what do you do for the company?" Then you find out that this person would be your boss—that is, if he or she were to hire you, which is probably doubtful at this point.

When your interview is arranged, ask for the names and titles of everyone you're going to meet with. If you are communicating with the recruiter or HR, ask if there is anything you should know about the interviewer. Then google every person you're going to meet. You need to find out everything you can about them so you can identify potential commonalities. These connections are hugely important because they establish common ground.

Academic researchers have done numerous studies about the "hire like me bias." It isn't just about gender, race, or ethnic background. It's also about such things as pedigree, that is, coming from the same socioeconomic class or sharing other backgrounds,

such as baseball, opera, dance, etc. That's not to defend these biases or claim that they're fair. But the fact is, humans do have unconscious biases and tend to gravitate toward people with whom they have commonalities.

Your job is to look for connection points: You share an alma mater, or you both worked for the same company several years ago. Those are the type of commonalities to mention as you sit down for the interview. Or your interviewer's LinkedIn profile might mention a personal interest in a social cause, sport, or activity. If you genuinely share that interest, it's another commonality to leverage. Just make sure it's a *real* interest of yours. If not, your lack of knowledge will become painfully clear, and you'll label yourself a "poser."

You also may find an icebreaker with the recruiter based on his or her profile. One candidate, noticing the recruiter's alma mater, made this comment: "I see you went to USC. That was a great Rose Bowl game last year."

If you can't find anything in the interviewer's profile, look for current themes: The company just announced a new product, or the CEO was recently on CNBC with positive news about the company. Even a benign observation—"I see that the company just made an acquisition. This must be a very exciting and busy time...."—can be an effective opener and conversation starter.

Also, when you walk into the interviewer's office or a conference room, look for points

> **Humans do have unconscious biases and tend to gravitate toward people with whom they have commonalities.**

of interest, just like you would if you were visiting someone's home for the first time.

One word of caution: Do not mention anything about the interviewer's personal life or family, at least not initially. Comments about a spouse or partner or the number or ages of children might be too personal at this point. However, if the interviewer asks you a personal question—such as "Where do you live?"—you can ask the same question. And if he or she mentions family, you can talk about yours. Remember, your goal is for your interview to be a conversation, not a Q&A.

THE SIXTH SIN
HAVING NO RELEVANT EXAMPLES OF YOUR ACCOMPLISHMENTS

The interviewer asks you to elaborate on the accomplishments you've listed on your resume, and because you're nervous, your mind goes blank. You stumble along, even reading from the copy of your resume you brought along. Unfortunately, the interviewer is listening for specifics to determine how you match the demands of the job and how well you would communicate with colleagues and customers.

The examples you give in your interview should cover four key areas: the challenge/opportunity faced, the actions taken, the results achieved, and the lessons learned

from the experience. Identify these examples ahead of time and practice relating them concisely and compellingly. Bullet them out in fifteen-second sound bites. Record yourself and listen to how well you deliver this information. You need to showcase what you've accomplished and how these experiences and lessons learned make you the perfect person for this job.

THE SEVENTH SIN
TALKING TOO MUCH OR TOO LITTLE

The interviewer asks you a question that you're not prepared to answer: "Tell me how you would handle this challenge..." In a panic, you do one of two things. Either you go on and on, hoping that you will say something relevant, or you give a short answer and then go silent. Or maybe you take a third tack: Hoping inspiration will strike, you stall for time by asking, "Can you repeat the question?"

Your best strategy is to prepare by rehearsing. Do a mock interview with a mentor or friend so you can practice giving your answers clearly and concisely. If nervousness tends to turn you into a statue, practice your presentation and your active listening by role-playing with a coach, mentor, or friend.

You don't want to memorize your lines or come across as scripted. And if you are asked a question that stumps you, it's perfectly acceptable for you to ask clarifying questions. Remember, it's a conversation. But the more you practice, the more fluently and fluidly you'll be able to present your experiences and achievements.

Be Prepared for Any of These Interview Scenarios

Sitting across the desk or conference room from your interviewer.

Sitting side by side, with no barriers (which makes your socks, length of trousers/skirt, and other details of your appearance so much more noticeable).

A roundtable with two or more interviewers, or having multiple conversations with people—some of them "on the fly."

THE EIGHTH SIN
HAVING NO MEANINGFUL QUESTIONS TO ASK

Midway through the interview, the hiring manager asks, "What questions can I answer for you?" Replying, "I'm good, thanks," as if someone had offered to refill your iced tea, shows a lack of preparedness and engagement.

You must prepare for the questions the interviewer will likely ask you, but equally important are the questions you ask the interviewer. Your questions should be smart and strategic, probing the job responsibilities or how the department functions. The questions you ask also show the interviewer how you think. By easily inserting your questions into the interview, you'll turn a one-way question-and-answer session into a conversation.

At the end of the interview, *do not* ask about "next steps" in the interview process. If you've done well in the interview, you'll be asked back soon enough. Instead, tell the interviewer how much you love the company, enjoyed the conversation, and are interested in the position. Demonstrate your interest in next steps by showing, saying, and believing!

THE NINTH SIN
APPEARING DESPERATE

Through nonverbal cues such as sitting on the edge of your chair, or by saying things like "I really need this job" or "When will I hear from you?" you can radiate desperation. That's only going to raise doubts in the interviewer's mind about your abilities, your fit with the organization, and why others haven't hired you.

Your nonverbal cues may be unconscious. Perhaps you're not aware of how often you fold your arms tightly against your body (which can make you appear

LOSE THE RESUME, LAND THE JOB

unfriendly or defensive) or that you frown when you listen. Video record a mock interview and watch yourself later. Do your verbal and nonverbal messages inspire confidence or trigger concern?

Don't send the wrong signal because you were clueless about how you appear to others.

Actions Speak Louder...

Just as important as *what* you say is *how* you say it. Be aware of your nonverbal cues and what they say to your interviewer.

Make eye contact You will appear more confident and friendlier. Avoid looking down. You'll appear distracted or lacking in confidence.

Arms free, not folded You'll project openness, while keeping your hands free to gesture.

Sitting forward/back Leaning forward (but not on the edge of your seat) helps you present your ideas. If you lean back while listening, make sure your posture stays open.

Standing Good posture, arms at your side, gives you confidence. Don't fidget or rock from side to side.

Smile Convey happiness and confidence—and make others feel good about themselves.

THE TENTH SIN
BEING INTERRUPTED BY A CALL, TEXT, OR EMAIL

Your phone going off during the interview is a short but especially lethal sin. Turn off your phone before you reach the front door of the building.

Should you forget, and your phone pings a message or rings with an incoming call, never answer it. When you are in an interview, nothing else matters.

THE ELEVENTH SIN
BRINGING SOMETHING TO DRINK (OR WORSE, TO EAT) INTO THE INTERVIEW

You may be offered water by the receptionist or the interviewer. If so, you may accept. In fact, you should ask to help, just as you would if you were a guest in someone's home. Where are the glasses kept? If there's a water pitcher on the table, offer to pour for your interviewer.

But never bring in something yourself: no coffee, soda, snack, or anything else. And yes, we did hear of someone who explained that she was on her lunch break and asked if she could eat while they talked.

THE TWELFTH SIN
NOT HAVING A "PLAN B" FOR YOUR VIDEO/SKYPE INTERVIEW

Interviewing is hard enough. Now add technology into the mix and you've got more to worry about: lost Internet connection, dropped signals. If your interview is by Skype or video conference, you have one more deadly sin to avoid: not preparing for what can (and probably will) go wrong.

VIDEO-CONFERENCE INTERVIEWS

If you are going to a video-conference location, arrive early so you can learn about equipment. Have a backup phone number and an email address in case of equipment failure. Be aware that some video-conference systems have a two- or three-second delay between the visual and the voice communication. Allow a little time in the give-and-take of the interview conversation.

SKYPE AND WEBCAM INTERVIEWS

Thoroughly test your side of things. For example, do you know your Skype password? You won't believe how many people have forgotten-password issues just as they're supposed to be logging in. As practice runs, Skype with a friend several times before the interview. Can you connect? How do you look? Do those extra chins show up less if you sit on a few pillows? Do you have great eyes that get lost when you're too far from the camera? How do you sound? The more you practice, the better you'll feel about using the technology.

If you are doing the interview via webcam at home, check the background and the foreground. I can remember doing a webcam interview with someone who had what looked like a liquor bottle on his desk. It turned out to be iced tea, but it was still a major distraction. The background should be a professional setting. Don't do a webcam interview in your bedroom with your closet door open, or in the kitchen with dishes on the counter. Check the lighting. Make sure there are no pets or other distractions in the room. Once again, a practice session with a friend on Skype can help you figure out the best setting, lighting, and angle of the webcam.

Dress for the interview, even if you think it's only "head and shoulders." You may not be planning to leave your chair during the interview, but what if you have to get up for some reason—to shut a door or a window because of noise (something you should do beforehand)? You don't want to reveal any surprises. This was a lesson learned too late for one webcam interviewee who from the waist up was all Brooks Brothers. But when his dog nudged the door open and he had to jump up to close it, the candidate revealed he was wearing only boxers.

Have a Plan B in case there's a power outage in your neighborhood, the Internet is down, or the street-maintenance crew is jackhammering outside. When you prepare for problems, it's far more likely that everything will go smoothly. ●

THE GREAT UNKNOWN: INTERVIEW QUESTIONS

The final part of your interview preparation goes to the heart of the matter: What you will say during the interview. The questions the interviewer asks may be the most mundane, or they could be zingers out of the blue. You can't possibly know how it will go—whether you'll be grilled with tough questions or you'll be asked the standard queries out of Interviewing 101.

While you can't control the questions, you do have a lot of control over your answers. You must prepare in advance. No matter what is asked—from the straightforward "What are your strengths?" to the bizarre "If you were an animal, what would you be?"—if you have solid answers and concise examples at the ready, you'll be prepared for just about anything.

As you address the following interview-prep questions and prompts, I suggest dumbing it down a little so your responses sound natural and conversational. Imagine talking to a fourteen-year-old.

INTERVIEW-PREP QUESTIONS & PROMPTS

TELL ME ABOUT YOURSELF.
Don't answer by reciting everything that's on your resume. Talk for about thirty seconds. Make it *conversational*. My suggestion is to start with something personal—where you were raised, where you went to school, your family, when you moved to your current city, why you went into the career you've chosen. Briefly summarize what you're passionate about.

TELL ME ABOUT YOUR MOST RECENT POSITION.
Be prepared to discuss what you're doing in a way that's relevant and applicable to the position you're seeking. Use brief stories to illustrate points: challenge, action, result, lessons learned.

WHAT'S YOUR GREATEST CAREER ACCOMPLISHMENT?
Giving a great answer to this question can get you the job. Tell a thirty-second story with details. Talk about a problem that was overcome or an opportunity that was realized.

WHAT ARE YOUR STRENGTHS?
Identify two or three strengths and discuss each with a specific example.

Focus on strengths that are the most relevant to the job you're seeking.

WHAT ARE YOUR WEAKNESSES?

Telling the interviewer that you "work too hard" or you "care too much" won't cut it. Companies want a real answer from you. Have a couple examples of areas that you're working on, maybe something you highlighted in your last job-performance appraisal (or weaknesses that were revealed in the assessment you took here, or on the KFAdvance site).

WHAT MAJOR PROBLEM, CHALLENGE, OR FAILURE HAVE YOU HAD TO OVERCOME, AND HOW DID YOU DO IT?

In addition to highlighting your skills and competencies in your answer, you can showcase your goal orientation, work ethic, personal commitment, and integrity. Overcoming numerous or significant difficulties to succeed requires these qualities. Demonstrate your resilience.

CAN YOU DESCRIBE A SITUATION IN WHICH YOU TOOK THE INITIATIVE TO ACCOMPLISH A GOAL?

Your interviewer is listening for examples of how you've been proactive and results oriented. Describe your motivation and when you made the extra effort and used your creativity to solve a problem or realize an opportunity.

WHY DO YOU WANT TO WORK HERE?

What do you know about the company? This is an opportunity for you to discuss the "fit factor": what you admire about the company, its mission and purpose, its products and services, and the culture.

WHAT VALUE DO YOU BRING?

Why should we hire you? Pick two or three main factors about the job and how you meet those qualifications. Discuss for one minute with specific details. Examples to highlight include your technical skills and your management skills that make you an excellent fit for the job. (For more-junior positions you'll probably spend more time talking about technical skills. But as you progress, you'll need to highlight how you work with, motivate, and manage others.)

WHERE DO YOU WANT TO BE IN FIVE YEARS?

Aspire, but be realistic. If your goals are too lofty, you'll come across as immature. One or two career moves in five years is reasonable.

YOUR MENTAL GAME

Preparing for the interview is more than half the battle. The more you know—about the company, its products, the culture, the job opportunity, the interviewer—the more confident you will feel, and the better chance you'll have of connecting with the interviewer. Instead of appearing nervous and anxious, like you're facing a geometry test you didn't study for, you'll come across as relaxed and prepared.

Don't psych yourself out! Focusing on your mental game will help you avoid mistakes and present yourself as smart and strategic. You'll have your ACT together, and with practice, it will become second nature. •

YOUR ACT IN ACTION

TEN

YOUR ACT IN ACTION

You're merging onto the highway. Looking over your left shoulder, you judge the pace of the traffic. You can't crawl along at twenty miles per hour, nor can you punch the accelerator and speed up to eighty. How fast or slow you proceed does not depend on you, but on everyone else on the road. To merge safely, you must literally go with the flow.

The same applies to your interview. No matter how much you prepare, you must adjust to the content and tempo set by the interviewer, and do it in real time. You may meet with an experienced and skilled interviewer who is very good at asking questions. Or you may find yourself across the desk from an incompetent interviewer who is disorganized and distracted. You can't plan for this. You have to go with the flow.

> **The Unspoken Truth**
>
> ✖
>
> **The interview is not about you. It's all about connecting with others.**

The good news is that having spent so much time preparing, you've increased your chances of success. You know who you are: You are highly aware of your strengths and weaknesses. This self-knowledge enables you to present yourself authentically. In addition, you've made the effort to know the company and its culture, how its employees dress, and the interviewer's background and interests. All these factors will help you forge a connection. Furthermore, having rehearsed your stories and examples, you are ready to describe your accomplishments in a way that's meaningful and relevant to the skills and expertise required in the position you're seeking.

This is your ACT in action.

But just remember that while your preparation was all about you, the interview itself isn't about you at all! It's about the hiring manager, the other team members, and every other person you meet.

I liken this dynamic to being a guest in someone's home for the first time. To show respect and make a connection with your hosts, you follow the protocol. You wipe your feet on the mat, probably taking more care than you do in your own house. Removing your shoes by the door, if that's the house rule, may make you feel a little uncomfortable, but you do it anyway. You are relaxed and smiling, offering your hand to shake. You take care where to sit, making sure you don't appear presumptuous by taking the host's favorite chair. You are patient and attentive. If beverages are served, you offer to help and never leave a glass or coffee cup for someone else to clean up. The conversation flows with the give-and-take of people getting to know each other.

In your interview, you follow the same visitor's protocol. Your focus in on your "host"—in this case, the interviewer. You smile and make eye contact. As you listen carefully to the questions, you pay attention to their pace and tempo, and you read the interviewer's tone and body language. If you're in sync with him or her, the exchange of information will feel much more relaxed—like a conversation and not an interrogation.

But not all interviewers are created equal. Some fire questions at you; others ramble without a clear point. It's up to you to be flexible and adaptable. No matter if the "host" is relaxed and welcoming, or gruff and guarded, you never stop being the gracious visitor. You constantly and consistently ACT. ●

THE FIVE INTERVIEWERS

Interviewing is a little like the Wild West: Everybody does things his or her own way. Some people stick by a standard Q&A script. Others do most of the talking. And some like to throw in an oddball question to see how you'll react. But the real wild card is the interviewer. Some hiring managers are very skilled at interviewing. Some do okay, and some are downright awful. In general, they fall into five categories based on their style and approach. You'll find these types of interviewers at every level and in every industry and company.

1 THE GENERAL

This interviewer takes a no-nonsense approach. The General will probably sit across from you, keeping something—his or her desk, the conference table—

between the two of you. That puts the General automatically in a power position, which may feel challenging to you. Direct, professional, and somewhat impersonal, the General is more interested in what you would bring to the job than in your personality. The General is likely to be an intimidating interviewer, asking concise questions and expecting concise answers.

Although you probably won't get much small talk from this interviewer at first, you should still look around the General's neat and well-organized office for possible connecting points. It could be a photograph, a piece of art—even the view out the window. The General may prefer succinct, results-oriented responses, but don't forget your "visitor behavior"—smiling, friendly, respectful. As you would be with any interviewer, you're prepared to relate brief anecdotes and examples that effectively translate how your experience meets the company's

needs. And don't forget to ask the General questions. This is a conversation, not a stand-and-deliver examination.

2 THE TALK SHOW HOST

This interviewer is all about making sure people like each other—and like him or her. The Talk Show Host will greet you warmly, go out of his or her way to make you comfortable, and will spend a lot of time in small talk. You'll most likely meet in an office that reveals this interviewer's style and personality: photos, art, mementos, and other glimpses into his or her personal life. The Talk Show Host will probably sit next to you, which can be disarming—and that's the whole point. You're more likely to let your guard down when you're sitting beside your interviewer. It's probably easiest to discuss personal interests as you forge a connection with

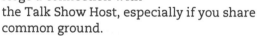

the Talk Show Host, especially if you share common ground.

The Talk Show Host is less concerned with the details of your experience and focuses more on how well you fit in with the company's culture and environment. This interviewer will speak of "we" and will emphasize commitment to the company. Respond in kind. Emphasize your people skills.

③ THE SCIENTIST

This analytical interviewer wants to know *how* you intend to contribute and is less interested in what you're doing now or have done. The Scientist appreciates lengthy, detailed answers and will probably be frustrated by answers that are too short or lacking specifics.

The Scientist is generally more personable than the General, but he or she is more direct than the Talk Show Host. (But don't forget your ACT. It is *always* your guide!) The Scientist is an effective decision-maker who makes an assessment from many facts; therefore, this interviewer responds particularly well to answers that include specific examples. He or she wants to determine how well you would do in the job, the kinds of skills and experiences you would apply to problems, and the kind of results you can deliver.

④ THE BUMBLER

This incompetent interviewer will likely ramble, appear disorganized, and may be unclear about the position you're interviewing for. Your best hope here is to take charge and provide structure for the meeting. In fact, as the "gracious visitor" in this interview, you share more of the "hosting" duties by volunteering information and directing the questions as best you can. As you proactively offer a summary of your skills and accomplishments, you can help the Bumbler ascertain the necessary information about you and your skill set.

⑤ THE CLUELESS

This interviewer admits right away to not having read your resume and may not even know what position you're interviewing for. When you hear "What job are you here for?" your heart may sink. But the Clueless manager isn't doing anything different from all the other interviewers. He or she is just more transparent about it. As stated earlier in the book, hiring managers spend only *seconds* in their initial screening of your resume. And even if they "study" resumes more closely, it likely involves less than five minutes of their time (and probably *much* less). For that reason alone, you should go into *every* interview with any *type* of interviewer assuming that he or she has not really read your resume.

Don't be frustrated. Just go with it. Stay grounded in your ACT, and seek to make a connection and establish an open and relaxed conversation. With this approach, even an interview with a Clueless manager can be a success. And you'll likely distinguish yourself for how you made the interviewer feel. ●

THE DETAILS

When I meet with someone, I prefer to sit side by side. It's more personable and welcoming. But it also puts the spotlight on small things, like the kaleidoscopic socks one guy wore. Once I noticed them, I couldn't stop seeing them in my peripheral vision. Whatever his reason for making such a fashion statement, the socks were a distraction—especially since we were meeting for the first time. Small details—socks, hemlines, polished shoes, snags and smudges—are very visible and suddenly matter a lot when you're sitting close together.

I Cannot Tell a Lie

$\left(\text{Except in the}\atop\text{Job Interview}\right)$

In this book, how many times have I told you not to lie? Yet a University of Massachusetts study that gained some notice found that a remarkable number of the participants— 81 percent—lied during a job interview.

81% LIE!

It worked out to 2.19 *lies per fifteen-minute interview!* Wow, you say. Of course, there are degrees of lying, and this was only one study. But keep it in mind when you're sitting in the interview. Know that the pressure of wanting a job can create unfortunate tendencies among even the best of us.

GOING WITH THE FLOW

An interview normally follows a certain flow through three basic stages: opening, mid-stage, and close. Let's look at each of these three stages and how they can enhance your ACT.

THE OPENING: AN INSTANT CONNECTION

Most candidates assume that their interview begins when the hiring manager comes out to the reception area to greet them, or when another staff member escorts them to the manager's office or a conference room. Guess again.

Your interview starts the minute you enter the corporate campus or building. That's why you must make it a point to be nice to everyone: the parking lot attendant, the security guard, the receptionist, the maintenance crew. Not only is it polite, but you are "on" every step of the way.

Smile and greet people in a friendly manner as you walk in the door, check in with security, and make your way to the reception desk. Understand that everyone you interact with, no matter how briefly or tangentially, is part of your "interview." No, they're not "plants" who are spying on you. But hiring managers frequently will ask the staff, "How many of you interacted with so-and-so today? What did you think?"

I've heard many stories of candidates

who were rude to the receptionist and for that reason alone were not asked back for a second interview. I also know of a candidate who was polite and respectful as she chatted with a custodian adjusting a vent in the waiting room near the CEO's office. When the custodian saw the CEO a few hours later, he remarked, "The woman who came in this morning was so nice—very interesting and easy to talk to." The CEO took that "recommendation" seriously.

Once your interview gets underway, an initial period is typically devoted to establishing rapport. This lasts longer than the first seven seconds of the interviewer's snap judgments about you. An interviewer may take from two to five minutes to establish rapport, often by engaging in small talk. For example, if you had to travel any distance, the interviewer may ask about your drive or your flight. Or the interviewer may make a comment about the weather. Respond in kind—again, just like you would if you were a guest in someone's home for the first time. This is an opportunity for you to show your authenticity through your confidence, poise, and professional presence. In actions and words, you demonstrate that you are genu-

inely interested in getting to know the other person—even more interested than "selling" your skill set, experience, and accomplishments for this job.

Also during this initial period, notice your surroundings. Something you see could be a perfect icebreaker to start the conversation. Let's say the hiring manager displays a piece of sports memorabilia that catches your eye. If you're a fan of that sport, it's an easy, good-natured connection to make. By the end of the initial phase, as the serious questions begin, you should feel a connection with your interviewer. If so, the feeling is probably mutual.

THE MID-STAGE:
A TASTE OF YOUR CONTRIBUTION

The mid-stage of your interview is the main event: the exchange of information about the way your background fits the company's needs as defined by the available opportunity. You and the interviewer engage in a give-and-take conversation in which you learn about each other. You demonstrate how you can contribute to the achievement of the organization's goals, while you also find out more about the position.

A Gracious Guest, Not a Faithful Dog

One of my colleagues told this story about himself from the earliest days of his career. It was his first interview for a job, and the hiring manager led him into the conference room. The view out the window was of the Pacific Ocean, and the sunlight was glinting on the surface of the water. When the manager went to the window, my colleague, then in his early twenties, followed him. He stood right beside the manager, literally at his elbow, and waited for whatever the manager was going to point out to him. "I'm just fixing the blinds; there's a lot of glare," the manager said. "You can sit down." Sheepishly, my colleague took his seat, a little embarrassed but a lot wiser about being a gracious guest and not a tagalong.

"IT'S A CONVERSATION, NOT AN INTERROGATION."

DO

- → **Chill out**
  - Keep your perspective
  - Have a picture of someone or something you love
- → **Be authentic**
- → **Engage the interviewer up front**
  - Know everything you can about who you are meeting
  - Identify commonalities
- → **Prepare thoroughly**
  - Do your homework—the company's background, products/services, leaders, current challenges
  - Know the culture
  - Have a short elevator pitch
- → **Formulate responses to likely questions**
- → **Project enthusiasm**
- → **Close strong by showing interest**

DON'T

- → **Be overly effusive or too deferential**
- → **Be arrogant**—assuming you know more than the interviewer does about the company, the role, or life in general
- → **Ramble or talk too much**
- → **Get too personal**
- → **Disparage your current job/company or former employers**
  - Your next employer wants you to come to them, not run away *from* something
- → **Be afraid to say, "I don't know"**

HOW CAN YOU STAND OUT?

Another way to add value during the mid-stage of the interview is to think more strategically about what distinguishes you for this role. Clearly you have the right qualifications; otherwise, the hiring manager would not have invited you in for an interview. But the competition is tough, so you have to assume that everyone you're up against is similarly qualified. Some perhaps are even more qualified.

You need to stand out in interviewers' minds as they get a taste of what it would be like to have you on their team and in their organization. One way is to pick up on perceptions or assumptions that people may have about you because of your profession or background. I'm not talking about negative perceptions. But even positive assumptions can be limiting if people think that's all you possess.

A perfect example is military leaders, who are known for being disciplined, loyal, and mission-oriented—all great traits valued by organizations. In an interview, a military veteran who showcases these expected qualities but also discusses and

> **Be aware of perceptions or assumptions that people may have about you because of your profession or background.**

demonstrates something *unexpected*—being a creative, out-of-the-box thinker, for example—would really stand out.

Or consider the example of someone who has a Harvard MBA—a very impressive credential. A smart candidate might balance that distinction with a show of genuine humility and a willingness to learn. He or she could do that by saying something like, "I'm always learning from everyone."

This concept also applies to other background/resume perceptions, such as the impression that you have been at a company for a long time, that you're a "job-hopper," that you have too many gaps in your employment history, etc. Be prepared to address such notions proactively—and authentically. Don't let someone else's perception become your reality.

Ultimately, the best way you can stand out is to show the hiring manager how you would add value to the organization. The manager has specific goals that must be achieved. Your objective in the interview is to show exactly how you can help achieve them—and make your new boss look good. •

ANSWERING THE UNEXPECTED

"How many basketballs would it take to fill this room?"

"How many quarters would it take to reach the top of the building?"

As part of the interview, you may be asked some unexpected questions. The interviewer isn't looking for a correct answer. Instead, he or she wants to probe your reactions, to see how you adapt to the unexpected. Most important, the interviewer wants to find out more about how you think.

How would you respond to the following questions?

Have you ever stolen anything from a hotel room? If so, what? (Is taking a pen from the nightstand considered stealing?)

What's the last book you read?

Who's your favorite musician?

What do you think about when you're driving?

Who's your role model?

When I've used this questioning strategy with interviewees, I'm often surprised by the reaction. Some people take out a piece of paper and do a few calculations to come up with an answer. Others puzzle it out and then make an educated guess. Some use a quirky question—"If you wrote a song, what would the title be?" or "How do you make a tuna fish sandwich?"— as an opportunity to tell a little story about themselves.

But some don't even try. They just stare or even complain, "Why would you ask me *that?*" They've completely missed the point: These oddball questions are about handling the unexpected, thinking creatively, and adjusting in the moment. These questions just might be the ticket to showcasing who you are and how well you'd fit in with the culture. ●

THE TOP 10
THINGS INTERVIEWERS ARE LOOKING FOR

1. **CULTURE FIT** The sense that you would work well with others in the company, department, or team

2. **MOTIVATION** What drives you to succeed

3. **SKILLS** Mostly technical skills for junior positions; management and leadership skills for more experienced executives

4. **LEADERSHIP POTENTIAL** How you lead yourself and others; your ability to be groomed for a leadership position one day

5. **COMMUNICATION SKILLS** Your speaking and *listening* abilities

6. **POISE AND APPEARANCE** How you present yourself; how customers or clients will experience you

7. **PROBLEM-SOLVING SKILLS** How adept you are at finding a solution by looking beyond the obvious or what's already being done

8. **INTERPERSONAL SKILLS** How you interact with others, how you make them feel

9. **WILLINGNESS TO ACCEPT RESPONSIBILITY** How you respond when you're tasked with trying to create the "new and different," and "failing fast" is to be expected

10. **WORKING WELL UNDER PRESSURE** Being able to handle workplace stress without losing your cool

Interviewers are looking for your ability to be groomed for a leadership position one day.

THE INTERVIEW CLOSE

At the end of the scheduled time, you will probably get the sense that the discussion is winding down. Your interviewer will start summarizing or could volunteer a little information about "next steps"—for example, coming in to meet other team members.

At this point, don't try to drag it on. Sure, the interview may have crucial stakes for you, but not for the hiring manager, who has others to see or needs to get back to work. At the same time, it's very important to restate, in short fashion, your interest in and enthusiasm for the job and establish the ground rules for what will follow. Summarize why you think you're a good fit for the organization. Ask the interviewer if there is anything else he or she would like to know about you or that you can elaborate on. Is there anything from the conversation that you can clarify? Does he or she have any questions about anything you said that you can answer now?

Finish strong by showing your interest in the position and your enthusiasm for the company, in your tone and with your body language. And then, to put it bluntly, get out. •

SAYING THANK YOU!

It's standard practice to send a note to your interviewer, thanking him or her for the opportunity and reiterating your interest in the position. Should it be an email or a handwritten note? Both. With an email, your response is received in real time. A handwritten note is a great follow-up and a personalized touch. But you can't always be sure that it makes it through the postal system and the mailroom. By sending both, you hedge your bets and make sure you've said "thank you."

One candidate for a management position wanted to ensure that his thank-you letter was received, so he sent it FedEx, even though the location was just across town. Deliverability was ensured, and there was a high probability that the envelope would be opened by the interviewer and not a staff member.

NEXT STEPS

If you are going to be called back for additional interviews, you'll find out soon. It will probably take the hiring manager a week or more to meet with other candidates and decide who among you will advance to the next round. The tough truth is that the longer you don't hear, the less likely you will. Don't put your life on hold. The competition is stiff, and no matter how much you might want the job, a great deal of the process is beyond your control. Continue your networking; keep pursuing other opportunities and talking to other companies.

If you are called back, you will likely meet with other members of the team—and be prepared for multiple rounds of interviews, even for a junior position. As the selection process continues, you may be given an assignment. For example, you could be asked to provide your thoughts about the role or the strategy. You may have to present a written document, make a presentation, or both.

At some point in the process, you may be given an assessment to determine your strengths and areas of development. Sophisticated companies may use the assessment results to tailor questions in follow-up interviews.

Don't be surprised if as part of your interviews with the team, you meet with a team member who is more junior than you are. Sometimes this surprises more-experienced individuals who don't

understand why they are meeting with someone who could be reporting to them. Often this is a way to probe culture fit. No matter the reason, keep up your ACT and interact with this person as if he or she is more senior than you. This is golden-rule time: Treat everyone the way you wish to be treated and you'll never go wrong.

One of the biggest challenges of multiple interviews is keeping things fresh for yourself. It's natural to begin to wonder, *Didn't I say that already?* I remember this feeling from my days in investment banking, when I was part of a road-show team doing investor presentations. Sometimes we'd meet with eight different investment groups in one day, fly at night to the next city, and start all over again in the morning. No matter that it was repetitive for us, we had to make each presentation seem as if it was the one and only.

The same applies to you when you're in the third or fourth (or more) round of interviews. Don't think you can skip the preamble because the various interviewers have already traded notes. When interviewer No. 6 asks you, "So, tell me about yourself," remember your ACT and answer the question like it's the first time you've heard it. ●

> **One of the biggest challenges of multiple interviews is keeping things fresh for yourself. It's natural to begin to wonder, *Didn't I say that already?***

Be Prepared For...

Assessments as part of the interview process, and for results to influence the questions you're asked in follow-up interviews (particularly in more sophisticated companies)

Drug tests, background checks, and criminal-history checks

Social-media scrutiny (as we discussed in Chapter Seven)

Also... Keep it fresh, always remaining aware of your ACT, and answering questions as if you're fielding them for the first time

Don't make assumptions; even if you make it all the way to finalist, you don't have the job yet

MEETING WITH SENIOR LEADERS

Depending on the level of the position you're interviewing for and the size of the company, you may meet with the CEO and/or other senior leaders.

In a small company, it would not be uncommon to meet with the CEO, even if you're interviewing for a junior position.

In larger companies, finalists for executive positions one and two steps down from the C level would likely be brought in to meet with the CEO.

Interviewees who would be direct reports to the CEO would likely meet with one or two members of the board of directors, in addition to the CEO.

Meeting with senior executives can be intimidating, especially if it's your first time. Just remember your ACT—especially being authentic. Over the years, I've had the opportunity to meet with presidents and prime ministers, celebrities and entertainers, CEOs of every size and type of company—all very impressive people. And I can remember my early days of meeting with executives much more senior than I was. My advice from all these experiences is to keep perspective. These individuals are not simply functions or titles; they're not gods, nor are they omnipotent. They are human beings with the same interests and stresses as everyone else. They have families; they want to be loved. Most are genuinely interested in others. Show respect. Be authentic. And don't forget, when you're brought in to meet a senior leader, it's just one person speaking to another. ●

THE OFFER

Now the moment has come—a job offer! It's a life-changing moment for you. The day may stick in mind for years to come. But don't be disappointed if the HR person or hiring manager seems only mildly excited. He or she is most likely focused on agreeing to a salary, duties, and a start date. If the job has been open for a long time, the HR person may well be under a lot of pressure to lock all this in quickly. It's usually easy to find out if this is true, and if it is, it can increase your leverage. What else should be running through your mind?

MAKE SURE YOU HAVE THE OFFER IN HAND
Don't negotiate against yourself by starting to ask for things before the company has made an offer. And don't respond to part of a verbal offer: "What do you think about X salary?" Instead, you can give a response

such as, "I would like to see that in the context of the overall employment offer. That way I don't keep coming back with questions and take up your time." Only respond to the company's formal written offer or, at a minimum, a term sheet.

PUT EVERYTHING ON THE TABLE AT ONCE
You don't want to discuss the elements piecemeal. If you keep coming back with "one more thing" to discuss, you'll frustrate the other party—and you may undermine the offer.

UNDERSTAND THE LEVERAGE YOU HAVE BEFORE YOU START
The company wants you and may very well be open to negotiating at least some elements of your compensation and employment terms and conditions. You might be

able to get more money, more vacation time, or other benefits. With senior positions, much more is negotiable, including sign-on bonuses (customary for positions paying low six figures and up), additional nonmonetary benefits, and make-whole payments to compensate for bonuses and other incentives being left behind at the soon-to-be-former employer.

With junior positions, you may have some leverage with pay, additional paid time off, or flexible work arrangements. Do not try to change your work arrangement after you've started working; negotiate up front to find out what's possible and acceptable to you and the employer. You will never have as much leverage as you do when the company makes the offer and wants you to join!

DO YOUR HOMEWORK AND KNOW THE VALUE OF THE JOB

Reasearch the market in which you are interviewing, as well as any premiums or bonuses that are applicable for someone at your level and experience. One of my colleagues gave the example of her daughter, an engineer and an Ivy League graduate who was negotiating an offer with an employer in Boston. The competitive regional job market and the young woman's pedigree resulted in a starting salary and bonus that were 30 percent higher than the original offer.

UNDERSTAND THAT COMPANIES HAVE COMPENSATION PHILOSOPHIES AND STRATEGIES

For a mid-level or senior position, a company may decide to pay a competitive salary—known as paying "at the median." Or a company may offer a lower salary—for example, at the twenty-fifth percentile of the range of comparable salaries for the same position across similar companies—and then offer more performance-based incentives. Conversely, the company may decide it needs to "pay up" for talent, particularly to recruit experienced external talent, and pay at the seventy-fifth percentile or even higher. Whatever the pay package, companies generally have a talent strategy that explains their compensation.

If you work in a city and state that allow a prospective employer to ask how much you're making now, don't inflate the figure. Telling the truth brings honesty, candor, and trust into the process.

GO INTO THE NEGOTIATION PROCESS WITH A VALUE MINDSET

Focus on the value you bring to helping the team, department, and/or company achieve its goals. The value mindset can keep you from coming off as arrogant or greedy, and it will prevent you from underselling yourself.

BE AWARE OF NON-COMPETE AGREEMENTS

Hopefully, you know about any limitations before you get this far into the process. But people sometimes discover, to their shock and dismay, that years ago they signed a non-compete agreement with their current employer that prohibits them from taking a position with a competitor. If this becomes an issue, you will probably need the services of an employment lawyer.

In addition, if your new employer wants you to sign a non-compete agreement, make sure you understand the terms and implications. The technology industry, in particular, has strict agreements. I recently met a Stanford engineering graduate who, in accepting a job with a leading technology firm right out of college, was required to sign a six-year contract with heavy non-compete and non-solicitation clauses. Don't just sign without understanding what the terms mean for your new job and your career going forward.

Remembering your ACT at every step played a huge role in landing this job.

But the bottom line, of course, is you now have what you want: a job. The hard work, I hope, was all worth it. Your friends and family are excited for you. You're going to give notice if you are working. If you're not working, maybe you're going to take one last vacation before you start. Job- and career-wise, is that it? Game, set, and match? Well, the short answer is no. Or let's hope not. Sure, having a job versus looking for one puts you in a totally different world and frame of mind. But if you noticed, remembering your ACT at every step of each phase played a huge role in landing this job. Now it must continue. ●

YOUR *NEXT* JOB

ELEVEN

YOUR *NEXT* JOB

Congratulations, you have a new job! Now it's time to think about the next one.

This might strike you as odd, given all you've gone through to land this new position. Your first inclination might be to take a break from all that "job-search stuff." Understandable—but unwise.

You're not looking to make a change immediately, not if you've followed the advice in this book and landed the right job. But there's no better way to advance your career than by distinguishing yourself in your brand-new job. And you heard it before and know it's true: The best time to find a new job is when you have a job.

So when do you get started? After all the work you've gone through to find a job, don't lose steam and focus on just the time off or vacation before the new position starts. How about contacting your new boss in advance to ask if there is any preparation you can do? Most bosses will say no, but it can't hurt to ask. Or you could use the time to learn about the company's structure, financials, and latest developments. You certainly don't want to be blindsided by news everyone else there knows: "You mean, she's *not* CEO anymore?" Nor do you want to come charging in the first day with a bunch of boneheaded suggestions that make your hiring manager wish she'd never offered you the job.

Do another culture check too, especially on dress code. "Overeager Sam," as we will call him, told me a story about how, on the first day of a new job, he wore his best Wall Street suit when he went to meet his boss, a division head, at one of the company's satellite offices. Sam didn't realize the dress code at the satellite office was more casual and was surprised when everyone who greeted him was wearing khakis. On the second day of work,

Your New Job Challenge: In every interaction with your colleagues, do they feel better after the conversation than they did before?

THE TOP 10 TIPS FOR YOUR NEW JOB

1
First impressions are forever—make them count.

2
Be the first one in and the last one out.

3
Be indispensable, particularly to your boss.

4
Be a learn-it-all.

5
Be known for expertise that nobody else in the company has.

6
Network, network, network.

7
Don't engage in watercooler gossip or talk poorly of others; take the high road, always.

8
Don't sap energy; energize others.

9
Think before you write; email has no context.

10
Be all-in, all the time; performance rises above the rest.

for a meeting with HR at headquarters a few miles away, he switched to his smartest-looking casual wear—he was really proud of the pink sweater—only to find everyone there neatly attired in business-professional wear that included ties and jackets.

For whatever reason, some of the hardest-working job hunters let their guard down when the gates to the firm are finally open. But the fact is, your career journey just advances to the new job. "The Top 10 Tips for Your New Job" (page 205) are some thoughts for the long run.

Your current job didn't come looking for you, and neither will your next one. But you can start advancing to that next job by onboarding with three basic strategies: becoming indispensable, especially to your boss; learning everything you can; and networking like it's a contact sport—and that means starting with the other person and what you can do for him or her. •

Looking, Always Looking

As mentioned earlier, the average tenure of a job keeps shrinking. It's down to less than five years for younger workers, who typically will have four jobs by the time they are thirty-two. Accepting this reality, more than half of the people who are satisfied with their jobs say they are "open" to a new one. Millennials, as you might expect, are even more accustomed to the new order of things: Some 70 percent who are satisfied with their jobs are nonetheless open to taking a new one.

BECOME INDISPENSABLE—ESPECIALLY TO YOUR BOSS

As you begin your work, forget about your job title or the technical description of your role. Your real job is all about one person: your boss. Yes, the boss—the person so many of us have trouble working with and even wrongly leave jobs over. Vow to yourself to make sure this relationship is perfect and be set on helping the boss succeed. We know what's at stake: Your boss has the biggest influence on your current job and on your future. He or she is the gateway to stretch assignments, new experiences, and promotions. Need help with a colleague? Want a new project? Is global experience your next logical step? It's the boss who makes it happen—or not.

The starting point (and boiling point) for any relationship, including the one with your new boss, is communication. I've found that many managers and some leaders are horrible communicators. Couple that with the fact that most new employees are somewhat intimidated by a new boss, and the result can be a disaster. Go into this relationship assuming your new boss won't clearly lay out his or her expectations, goals, or instructions. Approach this new relationship with humility—not timidity. Listen (don't just hear) to absorb the boss's message and its meaning, and ask clarifying questions to ensure you fully understand the expectations. Similarly, establish early "check-in" dates and a comfortable communication protocol. This will help ensure that you are not just meeting, but exceeding the boss's expectations, and that you're receiving constructive criticism. Believe it or not, in the real world you probably will not get feedback without asking for it. So ask for it.

For you to become indispensable to the boss, he or she also must be confident that you say what you mean and do what you say—on time and all the time. Watch your do-say ratio. Divide what you do by what you say. If the ratio is less than one-to-one, you've got a problem. In other words, treat your boss like a customer.

Finally, your boss hired you for a reason. Fulfill that reason and follow this simple advice: Don't be among the people who were hired for what they know and then get fired for who they are. Simply stated, don't be a jerk! •

> You can't be indispensable if you aren't focused on making your boss look good.

How to Have a Good Relationship with Your Boss

Deliver what you promise, on time and complete.

Be loyal to the boss and the team. Share credit and never engage in watercooler gossip.

Respect boundaries. Don't expect your boss to be your best friend.

Know how to disagree with your boss with honesty and candor.

Ask for periodic feedback, but don't constantly seek praise.

LEARN ALL YOU CAN

Be a learn-it-all! **The most important** reward from your new job—far more than salary, bonus, or title—is what you learn. One of the main reasons you took this new job (if you followed our earlier advice) is to gain new skills and expand your experiences. Now you must seize these opportunities so you can become a better contributor in your current job and position yourself for a promotion or a new job.

I have a favorite saying: "Knowledge is what you know. Wisdom is acknowledging what you don't know. Learning is the bridge between the two." Remember the 70-20-10 rule? It says that 70 percent of your learning and development will come from assignments that stretch you and allow you to learn new skills; 20 percent will be from other people, especially your boss; and 10 percent will be from training and courses. Avail yourself of every experience and chance to learn. Let your curiosity lead you, and commit to continuous learning.

Learning is all about adapting to the new and different—being open-minded and willing to find solutions that aren't obvious (when the tried-and-true is not so true anymore). As you advance in your career and become a leader, you'll need to retain your curiosity, which will keep you captivated and engaged. Leaders are known for being critical thinkers and able to handle complexity and ambiguity. Start developing these skills now. The more you learn, the more you will be able to accomplish. As you improve, so will those around you. Eventually, the entire organization will improve.

And by the way, to slow down all that job-hopping, the better companies put a lot of effort into offering training for

> **At every level, it's not simply about what you do, but also about what you learn.**

employees. Want a shocking number? I read that companies spent more than $70 billion on employee training in 2015 alone. So don't blow off that webinar from HR that seems deadly dull but will provide you with a critical skill set. (Does the name "Excel" come to mind?) Also, nearly 60 percent of companies in one survey said they were offering to pay employee tuition. ●

‖ NETWORK, NETWORK, NETWORK!

My biggest career lesson is that the world is indeed flat. Someone you know knows somebody who knows someone who knows someone who knows somebody who knows you! As I was writing this chapter, a Korn Ferry board member called me to say he had just interviewed a CEO candidate for a major U.S. restaurant chain. During the interview, the board member asked where the candidate lives. When the candidate mentioned a city in California, the board member replied, "My dearest friends, Bill and Lois Smith, live there." The candidate couldn't believe the coincidence. "Bill and Lois are my next-door neighbors."

Hearing this story, I could only hope, for the candidate's sake, that he brings in the

trash cans and that his dog doesn't make a mess on Bill's lawn.

The six degrees of separation—the idea that anyone can be connected to any other person through a chain of acquaintances with no more than five intermediaries—isn't just a theory in business and your career; it's a reality! Over my career, I've seen this played out thousands of times. Networking is about using these connections to your advantage. But the biggest misconception is that networking is about you. It's the opposite. It's about the other person.

As you start your new job, your networking should kick up a notch. For one thing, news of your job change will probably spread through your network, especially when you update your LinkedIn profile with your new job title and links to your new employer. You will probably receive some congratulatory emails—and some requests from people in your network for career advice based on how you landed your new job. They may be where you were at the start of this process: They want to change jobs but don't have a clue about how and where to start. Pay it forward! Your recent experience in the job market—what worked, what didn't, and the dos and don'ts of interviewing—will help the next person. This is another way to develop and enhance your network by focusing first on what you can give. You should be known as someone who's genuinely interested in others.

But that's not all. Your new company is a network. Approach it every day in that way. It will pay off in the long run, and in the short term there are huge payoffs. Companies have formal organizational charts, policies, and procedures. Yet in almost every company, there is a unique culture of how things are actually accomplished. I call this the *informal network*—the influencers, the people to whom you turn to get things done. Immediately talk to your peers to figure out this network: "Who are the influencers?" "How can I best work with her?" "What does he appreciate or dislike?"

Most people, though, don't think of their jobs this way. They walk around in a state of comfortable numbness (to paraphrase Pink Floyd). Instead of leading with their ACT, they give too little thought to the lasting impression they're making.

Such was the case with Beth, an operations manager at a midsize company where she had worked for several years. Then the

MANAGING FIRST IMPRESSIONS

As you start your job, you'll make a series of first impressions with your new colleagues. From how you dress to the way you treat people, you need to manage how others experience you.

Most people will try to make you feel welcome by showing you the ropes, answering questions, making sure you have what you need. Remember your "gracious guest" behavior as you acknowledge these efforts: Say please; thank everyone; do what you can to reciprocate. This may seem simple and even obvious, but it's shocking how many people start a new job thinking, *It's all about me.*

company was acquired by a larger firm, and things began to change. Because of her seniority, Beth assumed she was safe.

One day, two consultants came in to meet with Beth and others in her department. She brushed them off, saying she was too busy. Finally, she agreed to meet with them, at the insistence of her boss. But instead of giving them her undivided atten-

Most people give too little thought to the lasting impression they're making.

tion, Beth came to the meeting with food she'd brought from home and microwaved in the kitchen. Not only was the smell distracting, but she sat there with her head down, eating.

Flash forward about two months. As the integration of the two firms progressed, Beth's position was eliminated. Imagine the consultants' surprise when Beth tracked them down on LinkedIn and asked them to introduce her to other companies, because now she needed a job. The consultants made a couple of half-hearted attempts to help her, but didn't go out of their way. They weren't being unkind. Given how Beth had acted in the meeting, recommending her to other companies seemed like a risk to their reputations.

Moral of the story: No one has a crystal ball on his or her desk. You don't know what's going to happen—whether you're going to receive a surprise promotion or the unwelcome news of downsizing in your department. You cannot prevent things beyond your control. But if you become indispensable, learn all you can, and approach every interaction as a chance to network, you will come out on top. •

BE AN OUTLIER IN AN UNCERTAIN WORLD

In this ever-changing world, the one thing we can be sure about is that tomorrow won't look like today. *Globalization, digitization, automation*—these forces of progress are putting stresses on how and where we work. Some jobs that exist today will go the way of the blacksmith and the retail clerk. The way I see it, we're in the midst of a labor evolution—much like in the late 1800s. The ripples visible today are likely to become tides of significant change in the decades to come. How can you continue to be relevant? The answer is to be insatiably curious and be a learn-it-all.

Despite all the technological innovations of the past century, a simple truth remains: It takes talented people to make businesses successful and organizations great.

Companies everywhere will still need to attract, develop, and align people who represent a mosaic of talents and abilities—diverse by every definition. Inclusive organizations will embrace the multiplicity of differences as a competitive edge for understanding and serving global customers.

You want to be part of that mosaic. You want to stand out as being engaged in what you do. You don't want to go with the crowd—head down, drawn along by the current.

Allow me to share a story with you: Years ago, I went salmon fishing. It was a magnificent fall day. Towering trees with burgundy, yellow, and orange leaves shimmered against a blue sky. Wearing heavy waders, we stood thigh-high in the river, casting into the current. The salmon run was so plentiful that the fish literally bumped into us as they moved in one mass, following an instinctive urge to swim upstream.

Then suddenly, one fish broke above the surface. Strong and nimble, it made a perfect arc in the air—a "flying fish" out of its element. The sun caught the scales on its back, turning them shiny and iridescent.

I stood there watching in amazement, caught up in the beauty of this outlier. Something innate in this one fish—an individual among a streaming mass—made it rise above the complacency of the rest.

That image has stayed with me, a reminder of the temptation to float along "in the stream" with everyone else. Surrounded by so many others who are content to stay where they are, people can easily fall into the dangerous trap of doing what's enough, but not too much. They play it safe, never going beyond what's expected. They are the 80 percent who accomplish the 20 percent. The result is going with the flow, hooked by disengagement and entangled in nets of complacency.

What about you?

Are you willing to be an outlier, to be among the 20 percent who accomplish the 80 percent? Do you have the hunger to rise above the rest? These are not merely clever metaphors or rhetorical questions to contemplate. They go to the heart and soul of this book: No matter what tomorrow's workforce looks like, no matter what new "hot jobs" emerge, you need to "exercise" to grow in your career—to commit to self-improvement, to be agile and adaptable, and to learn. In other words, you need to take control.

I leave you with this: Rockets didn't take us to the moon; innovators did. Transformation isn't achieved by a machine; it takes the mind of a dreamer. ●

Rockets didn't take us to the moon; innovators did. Transformation isn't achieved by a machine; it takes the mind of a dreamer.

KNOW YOURSELF

Your KF4D Assessments

On the following pages, you will find three KF4D assessments to complement the discussion in Chapter Two:

- **Assessing Your Traits**
- **Assessing Your Drivers**
- **Assessing Your Competencies**

Each assessment is a valuable exercise that will help you know yourself better. Keep an open mind. You may be surprised by what you learn!

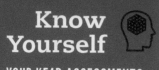
Score yourself on questions 2, 5, 7, 8, 11, and 12

4 points
STRONGLY
DISAGREE ▶

3 points
DISAGREE ▶

2 points
AGREE ▶

1 point
STRONGLY
AGREE ▶

Score yourself on questions 1, 3, 4, 6, 9, and 10

1 point
STRONGLY
DISAGREE ▶

2 points
DISAGREE ▶

3 points
AGREE ▶

4 points
STRONGLY
AGREE ▶

Assessing Your Traits

1 I UNDERSTAND PEOPLE'S FEELINGS AND MOTIVES. [ ]

2 I FOCUS ON THE FUTURE OR PAST MORE THAN THE PRESENT. [ ]

3 I STRIVE TO ACHIEVE LOFTY GOALS. [ ]

4 WHAT HAPPENS TO ME DEPENDS MOSTLY ON MY OWN EFFORTS. [ ]

5 I TEND TO SEEK OUT PEOPLE WHO THINK THE WAY I DO. [ ]

6 I TEND TO GIVE PEOPLE THE BENEFIT OF THE DOUBT. [ ]

7 NEW IDEAS TAKE ME OFF COURSE. [ ]

8 I PREFER INDEPENDENT WORK. [ ]

9 I AM KNOWN FOR MOTIVATING OTHERS. [ ]

10 I GENERALLY EXPECT THINGS TO TURN OUT FOR THE BEST. [ ]

11 I'D RATHER NOT BE IN CHARGE. [ ]

12 MY WORK SUFFERS WHEN I AM STRESSED. [ ]

Presence

Add items 1, 9, and 11 and refer to the following descriptions.

0 TO 6 POINTS
Your pattern of scores indicates a predisposition toward rationality, leading by example, and deferring to others for direction. These characteristics are hallmarks of the "vital many" in organizations, and are sometimes associated with jobs whose tasks are repeatable, structured, and predictable. Interestingly, individuals working in administrative services, accounting, and manufacturing often show a similar pattern of scores.

7 TO 12 POINTS
Your pattern of scores indicates a predisposition toward social and emotional presence. You are likely to be viewed as sociable, persuasive, commanding, and poised. These characteristics are hallmarks of organizational leaders and high-level managers, and are typically associated with jobs whose tasks are novel and unpredictable and involve people management. Similar scores are often seen among individuals in communications, sales, marketing, retail, and executive management.

Agreeableness

Add items 5, 6, and 8 and refer to the descriptions below.

1 TO 6 POINTS
Your pattern of scores indicates a predisposition toward skepticism, social caution, and independence. Your preference for solo efforts may sometimes present challenges to promotion, but can be an advantage for roles that require limited or only prescriptive collaboration. Similar patterns of scores are typically seen among individuals working in public safety, manufacturing, and legal and administrative services.

7 TO 12 POINTS
Your pattern of scores indicates a tendency to be considerate, humble, collaborative, and inclusive, and to see people as generally trustworthy. These charac-

teristics are key to positive teamwork outcomes and are often strongly sought after by employers. Similar results are often seen for individuals working in human resources, marketing, consulting, research & development, and executive management.

Striving

Add items 3, 4, and 7 and refer to the descriptions below.

1 TO 6 POINTS
Your pattern of scores indicates an aversion to competition, a tendency to be opportunistic, and a predisposition toward believing that fate, luck, or uncontrollable forces play a large role in determining life outcomes. In general, this pattern is sometimes associated with increased creativity, but is not typical of upper-level managers and can create challenges to job satisfaction and commitment in any role. Similar patterns are often seen among individuals working in communications, customer service, administrative services, and especially creative roles.

7 TO 12 POINTS
Your pattern of scores indicates a predisposition toward achievement orientation, reliability, and persistence. You are likely to be viewed as hardworking, results driven, and dependable. You likely persist in the face of obstacles when pursuing goals. These characteristics are a key to success in any role and are seen at high levels among

successful incumbents across the management pipeline. Similar scores are typically seen in individuals working in executive-management roles, strategic planning, legal, marketing, and health care.

Positivity

Add items 2, 10, and 12 and refer to the descriptions below.

1 TO 6 POINTS
Your pattern of scores indicates a predisposition toward realism, emotional transparency, and rumination. A tendency to dwell on the past or future can be a key to learning from experience, but is also sometimes associated with elevated stress and anxiety. However, people may find it easy to know your mood, which can be refreshing and is sometimes needed in communication. Similar scores are often seen among individuals working in manufacturing, creative fields, communications, and sales.

7 TO 12 POINTS
Your pattern of scores indicates a tendency toward positivity, optimism, composure, and mindfulness. You may have a tendency to reserve judgment and "live in the moment," which can serve as a protection against stress and anxiety. Similar score patterns are typically seen among individuals working in public safety, health care, retail, and executive management.

Know Yourself

YOUR KF4D ASSESSMENTS

Add items 1, 4, 5, 7, 8, and 9 to calculate your promotion-focused score

Add items 2, 3, 6, 10, 11, and 12 to calculate your preservation-focused score

1 point
VERY
LITTLE ▶

2 points
LITTLE ▶

3 points
SOME ▶

4 points
VERY
MUCH ▶

Assessing Your Drivers

HOW MUCH ARE YOU MOTIVATED BY...

1 DEVELOPING AND PURSUING YOUR OWN VISION [ ]

2 WORKING WITH OTHERS TOWARD A COMMON GOAL [ ]

3 ACHIEVING A BALANCED AND MULTIFACETED LIFESTYLE [ ]

4 GAINING THE RESPECT AND RECOGNITION OF OTHERS [ ]

5 WINNING AGAINST TOUGH COMPETITION [ ]

6 PREDICTABILITY AND STABILITY [ ]

7 FREEDOM FROM ORGANIZATIONAL CONSTRAINTS [ ]

8 INFLUENCE AND POWER [ ]

9 NEW AND CHALLENGING ASSIGNMENTS [ ]

10 TRADITIONS AND CONSISTENCY [ ]

11 BELONGING AND ACCEPTANCE IN A GROUP [ ]

12 WORK/LIFE BALANCE [ ]

Compare your promotion-focused and preservation-focused scores to see which is higher. Then read the description of the higher driver for insights from similar responders (page 219).

Promotion-Focused Description

Your pattern of scores indicates promotion-focused motivational tendencies. This means that in work you typically seek and strive to *approach* desired circumstances, rather than avoid undesired circumstances. You are likely to experience eagerness with goal striving and joy with goal attainment. Individuals who are promotion focused tend to prefer challenging roles that allow opportunity for personal growth, upward mobility, and achievement. They may pursue the respect and recognition of others and/or tend toward an entrepreneurial spirit and approach to work, while preferring environments in which promotion and rewards are granted according to merit. Individuals working in creative roles are among the highest scorers on promotion-focused motives. Other high scorers often include executive managers, sales people, strategic planners, and financial-services professionals.

Preservation-Focused Description

Your pattern of scores indicates preservation-focused motivational tendencies. This means that in work you typically seek and strive to avoid undesired circumstances, rather than approach and strive for desired circumstances. Individuals who are preservation focused tend to strive for stability, reliability, and if possible, low stress at work. They are motivated by job security, achieving a well-rounded background lifestyle, structured and well-defined roles, and being part of a supportive group. They typically prefer jobs in which promotion and reward come via seniority and/or tenure. Individuals working in health care are among the highest scorers on preservation-focused motives. Other high scorers often include educators, lawyers, and people working in research & development and engineering.

Assessing Your Competencies

Score yourself on questions 1-14

1 point
NO
SKILL ▶

2 points
LOW
SKILL ▶

3 points
SKILLED ▶

4 points
VERY
SKILLED ▶

1 MANAGING CONFLICTS [ ]

2 HAVING A BROAD PERSPECTIVE [ ]

3 UNDERSTANDING THE BUSINESS [ ]

4 ENSURING ACCOUNTABILITY OF YOURSELF AND OTHERS [ ]

5 STAYING ENGAGED WHEN THINGS ARE UNCLEAR [ ]

6 ADDRESSING THE NEEDS OF MULTIPLE STAKEHOLDERS [ ]

7 MAKING AND EXECUTING PLANS [ ]

8 INSPIRING OTHERS [ ]

9 COLLABORATING [ ]

10 LEADING YOURSELF AND OTHERS THROUGH A CRISIS [ ]

11 COMMUNICATING EFFECTIVELY TO DIVERSE AUDIENCES [ ]

12 BUILDING EFFECTIVE TEAMS [ ]

13 DEVELOPING YOUR SKILLS, KNOWLEDGE, AND ABILITIES [ ]

14 DELEGATING AND REMOVING OBSTACLES TO GET WORK DONE [ ]

People Competencies

Add items 1, 8, 9, 11, and 12 and refer to the descriptions below.

HIGH SCORE >=15
High scorers on people competencies use communication skills along with interpersonal and organizational savvy to develop talent and navigate through organizations. High scores are notably associated with increased promotion likelihood and better performance in most roles. Job functions such as executive management, customer/client service, marketing, sales, and even information technology all tend to have individuals with elevated people competencies.

LOW SCORE <15
Low scorers on people competencies tend to prefer and do better working independently and in task-oriented ways. Technical and process-oriented roles are more common among

low scorers. Without strong people competencies, promotion can be difficult as can performance in many of today's organizations, which increasingly rely on collaboration, group efforts, and leadership via lateral influence. Lower scores are typically seen among accountants and administrative-services professionals.

Thought Competencies

Add items 2, 3, and 6 and refer to the descriptions below.

HIGH SCORE >=9
High scorers on thought competencies tend to combine business insight with broad and strategic thinking in ways that help them manage and deal with complexity. They tend toward innovation and well-informed organization-related decision making. As with people competencies, high scores in thought competencies are notably associated with increased promotion likelihood and better performance in most roles. Job functions such as executive management, strategic planning, financial services, marketing, research & development, and information technology all tend to be occupied by individuals with elevated thought competencies.

LOW SCORE <9
Low scorers on thought competencies tend to have a narrow perspective on work and organizational outcomes. They prefer tried-and-true methods and structured work environments with more rote tasks and less complexity. Without strong thought competencies,

promotion can be difficult as can performance in many of today's organizations, which are increasingly complex, fast paced, and change-oriented.

Results Competencies

Add items 4, 7, and 14 and refer to the descriptions below.

HIGH SCORE >=9
High scorers on results competencies tend to combine action orientation, resourcefulness, and effective planning to drive execution and results. They tend to value and demonstrate hard work and accountability of themselves and others. While high scores are markedly associated with increased promotion likelihood and better performance in virtually all roles, related skills are relatively easy to develop in many cases. Job functions such as executive management, strategic planning, sales, manufacturing, and operations tend to be occupied by individuals with notably elevated results competencies.

LOW SCORE <9
Low scorers on results competencies tend to have a steady, unfocused, and deferential approach to work. They defer to others to make plans, to ensure execution, and to maintain accountability within the organization. They may seem content or even complacent and are not driven by competition or high standards, and don't place value on exceeding expectations. Without strong results competencies, both promotion and performance can be difficult in most roles.

Self-Competencies

Add items 5, 10, and 13 and refer to the descriptions below.

HIGH SCORE >=9
High scorers on self-competencies tend to combine fast learning with resilience in ways that help them make the most of their experiences, including successes and failures. They tend to be adaptable and courageous, and able to manage and navigate ambiguous circumstances. As with other competencies, high scores are markedly associated with increased promotion likelihood and better performance in most roles. Unlike results competencies, however, many key self-competencies are scarce and relatively hard to develop. Job functions such as executive management, strategic planning, and creative roles tend to be occupied by individuals with notably elevated self-competencies.

LOW SCORE <9
Low scorers on self-competencies tend to have an inflexible and process-oriented approach to work, while preferring roles that are well structured, detail-oriented, and predictable. They may not learn effectively from experiences, especially failures, and they may fail to adapt to changing and/or diverse circumstances. They may lack resilience and fail in crisis situations. Without strong self-competencies, promotion can be difficult as can performance in many of today's organizations, which are increasingly complex and change-oriented, and characterized by periods of ambiguity in goals and solutions.

Resume Samples

To complement the discussion in Chapter Six, we've included resumes in four categories: mid-level professional, senior executive (C level), junior professional, and recent college graduate/workforce entrant. (People, companies, and positions are hypothetical and not meant to represent real individuals or organizations. Numbers and percentages are represented by "X" to show style and format.)

These resume samples are set in Helvetica, a sans-serif typeface chosen for readability. An alternate serif typeface such as Times New Roman may also be used. Your resume is a serious document, so avoid highly stylized typefaces (like script) that distract from the business at hand.

Pat Sample

888 South Boulevard, Apt 2121
Phoenix, AZ, 85001
Cell (600) 600-0000 / Home (600) 000-6600
pat.sample@sample.com

PROFESSIONAL SUMMARY

- Health care executive with 14 years of startup and global management consulting experience
- Deep industry expertise in payors and providers
- Experience in taking a startup from idea to profitability
- Led major strategic and operational initiatives for marquee health care companies

PROFESSIONAL EXPERIENCE

Health Line, Phoenix   **2013–Present**

Health care IT startup founded in 2010 by a group of Harvard alumni. Its technology platform is sold to payor organizations and enables them to compare providers using proprietary analytics.

Vice President, Product Development
- Member of the executive team, reporting to the CEO; one of the first 5 employees of the firm.
- Responsible for driving growth through the commercialization of products.

Select Achievements
- Defined client segments and economics. Developed data-driven sales process, resulting in XX new clients.
- Drove XX product concepts into client-ready solutions.
- Developed proprietary algorithms to support measurement of client impact.
- Formed alliances with strategic partners to further sales growth, accounting for $XX million in revenue.

Global Consulting Associates, Chicago   2009–2013

Strategy consulting group with X,XXX employees across XX offices in X countries.

Principal, Health Care
- Led strategy, M&A, and operational improvement initiatives for leading
  U.S. health systems.

Select Engagements
- Program lead for the $X billion Sensar acquisition by KNT, the 3rd largest U.S.
  health plan. Oversaw XX teams that identified $XXX million in run-rate synergies.
- Program lead for 3-way health system merger to create a $X billion statewide
  network in Texas.
- Led numerous strategy and business process reengineering engagements for
  leading health care companies.

Highland Partners Consulting, Dallas   2003–2009

*Boutique strategy and organizational consulting firm serving Fortune 100 clients with expertise
in consumer products and health care.*

Senior Associate, Strategy Consulting (2005–2009)
- Led multi-year strategy and turnaround assignments.
- Responsibility for a team of XX consultants/associates.

Associate, Talent & Organizational Consulting (2003–2005)

EDUCATION

Harvard University
MBA, 2003

Baylor University
B.A., Economics (Honors), 2001

Susan Sample

333 Garden Street
Princeton, NJ 08000
Home (222) 000-0000; Cell (333) 111-1111
Email: susan.sample@samplemail.com

PROFESSIONAL EXPERIENCE

Sentara Cosmetics, Princeton   2011–Present

High-end cosmetics company with $XXX million in revenue and X,XXX employees. At the time of hire, private-equity backed. Successful IPO in 2017.

Chief Executive Officer

- Hired by private equity firm to turn around company and accelerate growth.
- During tenure quadrupled enterprise value, grew sales by $XXX million and increased EBITDA by $XX million.

Lumeena Care, Seattle   2008–2011

Fifth largest manufacturer of personal care products in the U.S. ($XXX million in revenue and X,XXX employees). Operates as a subsidiary of The Bart Company.

Chief Marketing Officer and Head of Strategy

- Responsible for strategy, marketing, R&D, regulatory, consumer care, and M&A.
- Helped grow enterprise value by $XX million over 3 years.

Croft and Sharp, Cincinnati   2000–2008

NYSE: CAZ. Multinational personal care company with $X billion in global sales and XX,XXX employees.

Senior Vice President and General Manager, Cosmetics (2005–2008)

- Responsible for cosmetic lines with XX brands in X categories; $XXX million in sales.
- Improved annual sales growth by XX%.

Vice President, Eye Creams (2002–2005)

- Led eye creams division; increased sales and profits by X% and X%, respectively.
- Successfully launched 3 new product lines and led expansion into Latin America.

Senior Brand Manager, San Francisco (2000–2002)

- Repositioned two major brands, increasing sales by XX%.

American Consulting Group, San Francisco   **1996–2000**

Global strategy consulting firm with XX offices in XX countries.

Principal (1998–2000)
- Managed all aspects of client relationships and service delivery for Fortune 500 companies with focus on retail and consumer products.

Senior Associate (1996–1998)

Nutraceuticals Productions, Los Angeles   **1992–1994**

Privately owned consumer goods and nutrition company with $X billion in revenue and XX,XXX employees.

Research Analyst, Marketing

EDUCATION

Cornell University
MBA, 1996

University of California Los Angeles (UCLA)
B.A. in Psychology, 1992

Boards
- Active: Board Member, YWWA Princeton (2013–Present)
- Past: Children's Cancer Research Fund Ohio (2005–2008)

Other
- Winner "Forty under 40" (Marketing Category, 2005)
- Member of YPO (Young Presidents Organization)
- Member of the UCLA Women's Rowing Team (1989–1991)

Bruce Sample

1075 Magnolia St.
Atlanta, GA 30301
Cell: (404) 000-0000
Email: BruceSample@sample.com

PROFESSIONAL EXPERIENCE

Hogan Logistics & Transportation, Atlanta   2012–Present

Privately held intermodal logistics provider with $XXX million in annual sales and XX,XXX employees.

Chief Executive Officer (2014–Present)

Became the first non-family CEO.

- Delivered on growth strategy:
  - Revenue increased from $XXX million in 2014 to $XXX million in 2017.
  - EBITDA increased by XX% to $XX million.
- Successfully launched X new product lines, currently representing X% of revenue.

Chief Operating Officer (2012–2014)

- Digitized logistics infrastructure, resulting in cost savings of $XX million.
- Successfully completed a merger of equals with XYZ Logistics.

Personal Leave / Consulting   2010–2012

Took 15 months off to care for elderly parents; Continued to do consulting work for Supra Logistics.

Supra Logistics, Savannah, GA   2004–2010

Supra Logistics is $XXX million (revenue) subsidiary of Freight Forward, a UK-headquartered company.

Vice President (2006–2010)

Responsible for Supra's $XXX million contract logistics business.

- Restructured business; recruited new leadership team, resulting in sales growth of XX%.

Director of Purchasing, Miami (2004–2006)

- Reengineered and executed a new strategic plan for procurement, resulting in $X million in cost savings.

Hansen Foods, Denver   **1993–2004**

Second largest global food/beverage company with $XXX in sales and XXX,XXX employees.

Regional Foodservice Director (2001–2004)
  - Led turnaround of Midwest market. Full P&L accountability for $XX million territory.

Director of Purchasing, Non-Food Category   (1998–2001)
Category Manager / Senior Buyer   (1995–1998)
Manager, Facility Engineering   (1993–1995)

MILITARY EXPERIENCE

United States Army, Various Worldwide Locations   **1983–1993**

Served for 10 years in a variety of leadership roles with progressive responsibilities.
  - Executive Officer (Captain), XXX Branch.
  - Aide-de-Camp for Brigadier General of XX,XXX-soldier logistics organization.
  - Commander of transportation unit during Operations XYZ and ABC.
  - Awarded Bronze Star.

EDUCATION

U.S. Military Academy at West Point
B.S., Economics. Graduated in top 5% of class, 1983

Grace Sample

111 Sunset Drive
Boston, MA 02110
Email: Grace.Sample@sample.com
Cell: (777) 111-1111

PROFESSIONAL EXPERIENCE

Raleigh Development, Boston   **November 2014–Present**

National real estate developer with $X billion in properties.

Financial Project Manager

- Managed $XXX million of mixed-use real estate projects, from concept to completion.
- Analyzed potential real estate acquisitions across XX states, completing deals totaling $XXX million.
- Promoted to lead team of X development associates.
- Developed new valuation model that led to more than $XX million in savings for the company.

PXP Global Advisors, Boston   **July 2013–October 2014**

Global financial advisory firm; total assets under management $X.X billion.

Associate, Private Wealth Management

- Managed client services and communication.
- Researched new investment products for partners.

EDUCATION

Lehigh University, College of Business and Economics

B.S., Business Administration, Real Estate Finance Minor (GPA 3.9), 2013
Studied abroad at the University of Cape Town (South Africa) for 5 months (2012)

The American School in London

High School Diploma, U.S. Curriculum, 2009

Activities and Organizations

Lehigh University CBE Study Abroad Mentor Program
Co-founder and vice president; one of two students selected to start the CBE Study Abroad Mentor Program.

Lehigh University Basketball Club
Treasurer

Kappa Alpha Society, Pennsylvania Alpha Chapter
President

SKILLS

Series 66, Project Management Professional (PMP) Certification

Lee Sample

111 Everest Drive, Apt # 222
Arlington, VA 55555
Email: lsample@leesample.com
Cell: 411-000-0000

Social Media:
Twitter: @LeeSampleFashion
Instagram: LeeSampleFashion
Personal Website: http://leesample.aboutme
LinkedIn: https://www.linkedin.com/in/leesample

PROFESSIONAL EXPERIENCE

Lee Sample Fashion, LLC, Arlington, VA   2015–Present

Online fashion brand with annual sales of $X million and XX employees.
www.leesamplefashion.com

Co-Founder and CEO
- Developed worldwide fashion brand with XX,XXX Instagram and Twitter followers.
- Media and celebrity endorsements, including Viva, Glama, and ABCD.
- Closed XX partnerships with companies in the U.S., UK, India, and Russia.
- Company in process of being acquired by a leading Chinese fashion house (expected close of sale end of 2017).

Personal Gap Year   2014

Traveled to XX countries across Europe and Asia.

Dimension Brands, Washington, D.C.   June–December 2013

Leading advertising and branding firm.

Junior Brand Manager
- Launched social media activities for Dimension Brands.

Internships

Keisuki Fashion, New York

Intern, Summer of 2012

Donald Investment Management, Baltimore

Summer intern, 2010 and 2011 (3 months each)

EDUCATION

Johns Hopkins University

B.A., Economics, Minor in Engineering 2013

SKILLS

Fluent in Chinese (speaking and writing)

Stephanie Sample

123 W. 112 St.
New York, NY 12312
Cell: 212-111-1111
Stephanie.sample@sample.com
www.stephanie.sample.net

EDUCATION

Syracuse University
B.A. in Communications, Minor in Political Science (GPA 4.0)

Academic Honors Summa Cum Laude, Dean's List

WORK EXPERIENCE

NewPost.com, New York   October 2016–Present

Digital news site averaging XXX million page views per month.

Editorial Assistant – Political Desk
Part of editorial team covering state politics. Work closely with managing editor, participating in daily news meetings. Manage home page for NewPost/NY.com website, coordinating social media and monitor traffic.

INTERNSHIPS

HallinganPolitics.com, New York   June–October 2016

Popular political news blog (owned by Big Media LLC).

Editorial Intern
- Assisted in all facets of news reporting, writing, and editing, including for award-winning SpotCheck investigative team.

WNNY, Syracuse   January–May 2016

Local XYZ News affiliate station.

Production Intern
- Assisted production team; worked on WNNY.com website.

Relevant Skills and Extracurricular Activities
Proficient in Spanish; Spent two summers (2014 and 2015) with America Serves Student Volunteers in infant/mother wellness program in Dominican Republic.

President of Beta Gamma Beta Sorority

INTERVIEWING
Advice and Insight

To supplement the discussion in Chapters Nine and Ten, we've included advice and insight—drawn from Korn Ferry expertise—about typical interview practices and common mistakes.

THE COMMON ELEMENTS OF A JOB INTERVIEW

IT DOESN'T LAST VERY LONG

The average interview lasts just under forty minutes. Even more interesting, a recent study showed the standard deviation (plus-or-minus variation) was twenty-five minutes. This means only a small percentage of interviews are longer than an hour—and it wouldn't be out of the ordinary for an interview to last only about fifteen minutes.

ROUGHLY EQUAL ATTENTION IS GIVEN TO DELIVERING AND GATHERING INFORMATION

In most organizations, interviews have a dual function: They are part opportunity to size up potential employees and part opportunity to sell the candidate on the organization.

THE TONE IS OFTEN INFORMAL AND UNSTRUCTURED

Typically, much of the interview focuses on building rapport and developing a good "feel" for the candidate. In doing so, the conversation can often flow from one topic to another, depending on the interests of either party.

THE CONTENT FROM INTERVIEW TO INTERVIEW IS INCONSISTENT

An interviewer often resorts to a small subset of standard questions he or she uses with every candidate. Aside from those questions, the content of an interview is likely to vary, depending on the candidate's background and what topics come up during the conversation. Even interviews for the same position may vary in content, which can make comparing candidates difficult.

NOTE TAKING IS LIMITED

Some interviewers naturally take copious notes. The majority, though, like to record a few observations or underline note-worthy information here and there on the resume. Long stretches of time can pass without the interviewer taking any notes.

The primary focus is often on technical abilities and individual achievements. Once they have an intuitive sense that they can work with a person, interviewers often shift their attention to determining if the individual has the requisite skills and abilities to perform the job on a day-to-day basis. Thus, they focus more on the candidate's knowledge base and track record of accomplishments than on such factors as strategic-thinking skills or the candidate's ability to get work done through others or to handle difficult situations with courage and composure.

WHAT HIRING MANAGERS ARE LOOKING FOR

We turned to the experts within Korn Ferry and the Korn Ferry Interview Architect, and through this lens we examined what employers are looking for in mid-level leaders and business-unit leaders. Note that while the profiles of mid-level leaders and business-unit leaders include some small differences, they are similar enough for us to combine them in one discussion.

WHAT GETS YOU IN THE DOOR

This is the baseline of skills and competencies that mid-level leaders and business-unit leaders are expected to have.

Possessing these skills and competencies doesn't make someone special; it just gets the candidate in the door to be considered along with all the other qualified people.

ENSURES ACCOUNTABILITY
Holding yourself and others accountable to meet commitments.

COLLABORATES
Building partnerships and working collaboratively with others to meet shared objectives.

DECISION QUALITY
Making good and timely decisions that keep the organization moving forward.

RESOURCEFULNESS
Securing and deploying resources effectively and efficiently.

COMMUNICATES EFFECTIVELY
Developing and delivering multimode communications that convey a clear understanding of the unique needs of different audiences.

HOW YOU SHOWCASE YOURSELF

The next set of skills and competencies defines the "competitive edge." Based on our research, this is what interviewers are most likely going to look for—and where candidates for mid-level or business-unit-leader positions can distinguish themselves.

ATTRACTS TOP TALENT
Attracting and selecting the best talent to meet current and future business needs.

DRIVES ENGAGEMENT
Creating a climate in which people are motivated to do their best to help the organization achieve its objectives.

DEMONSTRATES SELF-AWARENESS
Using a combination of feedback and reflection to gain productive insight into personal strengths and weaknesses.

OPTIMIZES WORK PROCESSES
Knowing the most effective and efficient processes to get things done, with a focus on continuous improvement.

GLOBAL PERSPECTIVE
Taking a broad view when approaching issues; using a global lens.

SELF-DEVELOPMENT
Actively seeking new ways to grow and be challenged using both formal and informal development channels.

BUSINESS INSIGHT
Applying knowledge of business and the marketplace to advance the organization's goals.

MANAGES COMPLEXITY
Making sense of complex, high-quantity, and sometimes contradictory information to effectively solve problems.

NIMBLE LEARNING
Actively learning through experimentation when tackling new problems; using both successes and failures as learning fodder.

BEING RESILIENT
Rebounding from setbacks and adversity when facing difficult situations.

HOW YOU STAND OUT

The top-level skills and competencies are the differentiators, and they are rarer and harder to develop. Mid-level and business-unit leaders who possess these capabilities or who show potential in these areas are more likely to stand out above the rest.

MANAGES CONFLICT
Handling conflict situations effectively, with a minimum of noise.

CULTIVATES INNOVATION
Creating new and better ways for the organization to be successful.

SITUATIONAL ADAPTABILITY
Adapting approach and demeanor in real time to match the shifting demands of different situations.

STRATEGIC MINDSET
Seeing ahead to future possibilities and translating them into breakthrough strategies.

BUILDS EFFECTIVE TEAMS
Building teams that apply their diverse skills and perspectives to achieve common goals.

MANAGES AMBIGUITY
Operating effectively, even when things are not certain or the way forward is not clear.

BUILDS NETWORKS
Effectively building formal and informal relationship networks inside and outside the organization.

DEVELOPS TALENT
Developing people to meet their career goals and the organization's goals.

DRIVES VISION AND PURPOSE
Painting a competitive picture of the vision and strategy that motivates others to action.

COURAGE
Stepping up to address difficult issues; saying what needs to be said.

VALUES DIFFERENCES
Recognizing the value that different perspectives and cultures bring to an organization.

INTERPERSONAL SAVVY
Relating openly and comfortably with diverse groups of people.

PERSUADES
Using compelling arguments to gain the support and commitment of others. •

A 360-DEGREE APPROACH TO ADVANCING YOUR CAREER

At Korn Ferry, we have shown 8 million executives how to achieve their career goals. Now, drawing on more than fifty years of award-winning expertise, we're offering a new solution to help people like you: KF Advance.

KF Advance offers a 360-degree approach to professional advancement. We leverage decades of expertise in executive search, assessment, learning and leadership development, and salary negotiation to help people pursue rewarding professional opportunities.

Our program is customized to you and your goals—while giving you access to the collective knowledge of Korn Ferry's more than 7,000 human-capital experts. Your KF Advance membership includes:

ONE-ON-ONE CAREER ADVANCEMENT

Work with the best in the business. Korn Ferry consultants place a candidate in a new role every three minutes and develop thousands of executives and professionals every month, so we know exactly what organizations want. You'll work with a personal advisor who provides customized strategies to guide you up the career ladder.

SELF-IMPROVEMENT

KF Advance offers an in-depth look at your traits, skills, and blind spots. In addition, by applying insights from your assessments, we analyze your fit within your job function, and help you capitalize on your strengths and style and create development plans beyond your current career trajectory.

RESUME IMPACT

Create a high-impact resume that attracts attention. Resume Architect runs your resume through today's latest resume-parsing technology, then helps you to build one that's less likely to be screened out by a recruiter or even worse, an automated resume system.

CUSTOMIZED INTERVIEWING FEEDBACK

After assessing your interview style, an interview expert will give you tailored feedback on how to prepare and polish yourself. This is the feedback you need to make the most of interviews that will lead to your next job.

JOB FINDER

Access a private job board of more than 2 million current opportunities. Every job posted on our exclusive platform comes directly from an employer looking to hire a person like you.

KORN FERRY ADVANCE PAY CHECK

With your job and market in mind, a Korn Ferry pay expert will leverage 20 million data points in our world-leading pay database to help you. Whether you're transitioning to a new role or preparing for your annual review, we arm you with the remuneration data you need to understand your value and get the most out of your pay and benefits.

Learn more about KF Advance: **KFAdvance.com** and **KFAdvance.com/losetheresume**

ACKNOWLEDGMENTS

Sitting over lunch at a deli one day, we hashed out an idea for a book on how to get a job—not the usual advice that everybody spouts off, but what it *really* takes. All of us could name countless people who are well intentioned, but absolutely clueless. These people need the tough love and unvarnished truth that no one—not spouses, partners, mentors, or anyone else—will tell them.

We loved the idea and immediately sought to test it out. In that moment, our waiter came over to take our order. Instead, we explained the concept and showed him three possible titles we'd just sketched out on the back of the specials-of-the-day card. "*Lose the Resume*—that says it all," he agreed, then went off to get our drinks.

A short while later—after his boss chewed him out over clearing multiple tables, while balancing orders for what seemed like half the restaurant—our overworked waiter returned. He leaned in and whispered, "When can I get this book? I'm looking for a new job."

This book is dedicated to all the hardworking waiters, office workers, sales associates, nurses, teachers, consultants, managers, and other professionals who hate their boss, whose talents are underused, and who feel unappreciated in what they do—but are still motivated to make a difference. There's hope.

My special thanks go to Dan Gugler, Patricia Crisafulli, and Jonathan Dahl, whose hard work is evident on these pages, and to Dana Martin Polk, for helping keep the process running smoothly. Many thanks to Robert Ross and Roland Madrid of RossMadrid for the design and layout of these pages.

I also want to acknowledge the invaluable help and insights of Kevin Cashman, Stu Crandell, Kate Kohler, James Lewis, Bill Sebra, and Inga Walter.

In addition, many people reached out with support, insights, enthusiasm, and stories.** Without each of you—and indeed, without every one of the nearly 8,000 people worldwide at Korn Ferry—this book would not have been possible.

Bryan Ackermann	Franz Gilbert
Scott Adams	Pablo Golfari
Liz Allison	Samantha Goodman
Cosme Almada	Varun Sampath Gorur
Rick Arons	Kasey Harboe Guentert
Juliana Barela	Matt Gurin
Katie Bell	Ken Hamada
Marianne Blair	Peri Hansen
Kenneth Bloom	Lisa-Marie Hanson
Adam Blumberg	Clarke Havener
Kari Browne	Chad Hesters
Adam Burden	Carolee Heynen
Cheryl Buxton	Bonnie Holub
Michele Capra	Christine Huang
Doug Charles	Brad Jardine
Bryan Davies	Mwamba Kasanda
Mhorag Doig	Peter Keseric
Chuck Eldridge	Ross Kirkham
Janet Feldman	Ira Krinsky
Brie Fifer	Jonathan Kuai
Christine Fuchs	Leonardo Lacruz

Beau Lambert	Igor Schmidt
Kherray Lim	Carrie Shapiro
Cody Loveland	Nicola Shocket
Tony Malinauskas	Carlos Alberto Silva
Georgia Matters	Bill Simon
Thomas McMullen	Ariane Soule
Stuart Melaia	Troy Steece
Rachel O'Connor	Seth Steinberg
Bruce Peterson	Craig Stephenson
Emilie Petrone	Michelle Stuntz
Hilary Pienaar	Brian Suh
Raj Ramachandran	Nicky Unsworth
Barbara Ramos	Caroline Vang
Bernadette Rigney	Eric van Zelm
Beatriz Rivera	Jonathan Vargas
Emily Robinson	George Vollmer
Rich Russo	Selena Yuan
Brett Ryder	Jake Zabkowicz
Steve Safier	Ron Zera
Elizabeth Schaefer	

** All the stories in this book are true or true-to-life.
The names and details (including the sample resumes) have
been changed to protect the innocent, the guilty,
and everyone in between.

NOTES